PRAISE FOR *VISUAL THEOLOGY*

Tim Challies (the writer) and Josh Byers (the designer) have teamed up to produce a truly unique introduction to theology and guide to living the Christian life. This is show-and-tell at its finest. Most theology books merely convey what we are to believe, but this one uses creative and beautiful design to capture and portray these crucial truths. I know of nothing else quite like it, and I trust that God will use it to help his people see and celebrate reality in a new way.

JUSTIN TAYLOR, managing editor of the *ESV Study Bible* and coauthor of *The Final Days of Jesus*

This is simple yet profound, clever without being flashy. Helpful and practical. Speaking as a person who avoids diagrams and graphs at all costs, I found the infographics in this book to be illuminating. This cheeky little number is a class act.

MEZ MCCONNELL, pastor of Niddrie Community Church, Edinburgh, and director of 20schemes

You've probably seen (or used) a gospel presentation drawn on a whiteboard or a napkin. It's remarkable how God gives us spiritual insight when we behold truths about him with our eyes. With engaging graphics and descriptions of the Christian faith, Tim Challies and Josh Byers have done something genuinely unique in *Visual Theology*. See for yourself!

GLORIA FURMAN, author of *Treasuring Christ When Your Hands Are Full* and *The Pastor's Wife*

My mind is blown. Tim Challies and Josh Byers marry rock-ribbed Reformational theology with breathtaking presentations. The effect is something like following John Knox into the Matrix. In this diaphanous world, we encounter no fiction, but very reality itself—God-reality—and we are transformed.

OWEN STRACHAN, associate professor of Christian theology and director of the Center on Gospel and Culture at Midwestern Baptist Theological Seminary

VISUAL
THEOLOGY

VISUAL THEOLOGY

SEEING AND UNDERSTANDING
THE TRUTH ABOUT GOD

TIM CHALLIES AND JOSH BYERS

ZONDERVAN

Visual Theology
Copyright © 2016 by Tim Challies and Josh Byers

This title is also available as a Zondervan ebook. Visit www.zondervan.com/ebooks.

Requests for information should be addressed to:
Zondervan, 3900 *Sparks Dr. SE, Grand Rapids, Michigan* 49546

Library of Congress Cataloging-in-Publication Data

Challies, Tim, 1976-
    Visual theology : seeing and understanding the truth about God / Tim Challies and Josh Byers.
      pages cm.
    ISBN 978-0-310-52043-6 (softcover)
    1. Theology, Doctrinal—Popular works. 2. Theology. 3. Christian life. I. Title.
    BT77.C4526 2016
    230.00—dc23   2015031836

Published in association with the literary agency of Wolgemuth & Associates, Inc.

Cover design: Studio Gearbox
Interior design and illustrations: Josh Byers

Printed in the United States of America

16 17 18 19 20 21 22 23 24 25 26 /DCI/ 20 19 18 17 16 15 14 13 12 11 10 9 8 7 6 5 4

CONTENTS

FOREWORD

*V*isual Theology is a delightful read. It combines wise knowledge of sound theology with a readable, inviting style and frequent perceptive insights into practical Christian living. Tim Challies and Josh Byers repeatedly tie their discussion to relevant Scripture passages and then provide a healthy and balanced application to the Christian life.

Another strength of this book is that it takes sin seriously, an emphasis that is sadly lacking in some evangelical writing and preaching today. This book describes practical steps for progressively overcoming sinful habits and patterns in the daily lives of Christians, something that is essential if we are going to grow in Christian maturity.

I often draw diagrams in the classroom because I find that students can more quickly grasp and retain theological concepts when they can see them in a single visual image. But this book has expanded that process far beyond anything I have ever done. The visually inviting infographics in this book are very helpful in synthesizing theological concepts and showing their application to practical Christian living.

I am happy to commend this book, and I expect that it will invite many readers on a pathway toward regular Christian growth and increasing likeness to our Lord Jesus Christ.

WAYNE GRUDEM, author of *Systematic Theology* and research professor
of theology and biblical studies at Phoenix Seminary

INTRODUCTION

I knew there would never be a better time than right now. I certainly wasn't getting any younger. Forty was closing in fast, and I wasn't getting any thinner, so I did the unthinkable: I walked into a health club and asked for help. "I want to not die. Can you help me with that?"

I had never seen the inside of a gym before. It was full of strange equipment being used in strange ways. Looking around, I saw athletic people showing off their strength and agility, lifting heavy things and twisting themselves into impossible positions. They all appeared so confident and so fit. I felt awkward, weak, and pathetic in comparison.

I got a glimpse that day of what it feels like to be in a strange and unusual place where everyone knows what to do and how things work, and you feel like an intruder. For many people, this is what it is like to walk into church for the very first time. You are convinced that everyone else is looking your way and muttering to their friends and neighbors, "He doesn't belong here …"

I stuck it out at the gym, in case you were wondering. They paired me with a trainer who evaluated me, created a program for me, and patiently showed me how to use all of that equipment. Over time, and through a dogged commitment to his program, I got results. I increased in strength, in stamina, in agility, and in health. And as an added benefit, I learned why the Bible calls every Christian to think of himself as an athlete.

Nearly two thousand years ago, a man named Paul, one of the earliest Christians, wrote to his young protégé Timothy and gave him this instruction: "Train yourself for godliness" (1 Timothy 4:7). Paul looked to the world of athletics, and there he found a fitting metaphor for the Christian life. Paul imagined the Christian as a kind of spiritual athlete, a person with a longing for spiritual fitness and spiritual success. Where an athlete strives for speed or strength, the Christian strives for godliness.

Godliness is a simple word, but hiding behind it is a lifelong challenge. The Bible sets before us two ways to live. The first way is to live a life that is consistent with God's desires and God's instructions. The second is to live a life that is consistent with our own desires and our own instructions. The great challenge laid before each Christian is to constantly grow in consistency with what God requires — to pursue growth that continues from the moment of salvation to the moment of death.

That is what this book is about. It is a book about growing in godliness. It is a book about how to live the Christian life and how to train yourself not just by believing the right doctrines and truth but by putting those beliefs into action. It will teach you how to live as a Christian; it will teach you how to assess yourself; and it will help you put together a plan to continue to grow throughout all of life. If an athlete disciplines himself until he breaks the ribbon and raises the trophy, the Christian disciplines himself until his life is over and he has received his eternal reward.

Just before Paul died, he wrote to Timothy once more and said, "I have fought the good fight, I have finished the race, I have kept the faith. Henceforth there is laid up for me the crown of righteousness, which the Lord, the righteous judge, will award to me on that Day, and not only to me but also to all who have loved his appearing" (2 Timothy 4:7 – 8). Every Christian longs to see and to receive that sweet crown of victory.

SPIRITUAL HEALTH

If a physical training program is going to make you healthy, it will emphasize a well-balanced view of fitness. If you lift weights and do nothing else, you may develop strong muscles, but you will not be fully healthy because your stamina will be unaffected. If you run on the treadmill but never learn to stretch or lift weights, you may develop stamina, but you will not be strong or flexible. You can be massively overdeveloped in some areas and pathetically underdeveloped in others. Healthy people are healthy all over. Healthy Christians are healthy all over too. God intends that we grow in balanced and coordinated ways. Let me explain what I mean.

We have all encountered Christians who have massive knowledge about Jesus but who don't seem to act much like Jesus. Yet we also know of some people who love to serve like Jesus served but who don't seem to have much knowledge of the Jesus the Bible reveals. Here, too, people can be overdeveloped in some areas and underdeveloped in others. The best-lived Christian life is one of discipline and coordination.

If we take all that we do and all that we are as Christians, we can divide the Christian life into four pursuits or disciplines. This book is structured around these four parts.[1] As Christians, we need to:

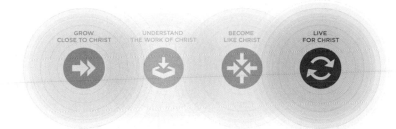

GROW CLOSE TO CHRIST

One thing that distinguishes Christianity from every other faith in the world is that Christianity is not only a religion but also a relationship. Some have repeated this so often that it can begin to sound trite or cliché, but let's not lose the wonder of this marvelous fact: Christianity is a religion based on a relationship with a person. As Christians, we have entered into a real and living relationship with the Creator of the universe. And as Christians, our first and most basic discipline is cultivating and growing into that personal relationship with Jesus as we hear from him, speak to him, and worship him.

UNDERSTAND THE WORK OF CHRIST

The Christian faith involves a relationship, but a relationship requires knowing things about the person as well, especially who they are and what they love to do. So there is also an essential content dimension to the Christian faith—information we need to know and facts we need to understand. Our emphasis in this second discipline is primarily on understanding the work of Christ. We need to grow in our understanding of what God is accomplishing in this world through the work of Christ. As we do that, we will also grow in our knowledge of God himself so we can better understand who he is and what he is like.

BECOME LIKE CHRIST

As we grow close to Christ and as we grow in our knowledge of his work, we will find ourselves with a longing to become like him. The Bible tells us that our purpose in life is to be conformed to his image — to think like him, to speak like him, to behave like him. We do this by putting away old habits, patterns, and passions and by replacing them with new and better habits, patterns, and passions. This will be the emphasis in the book's third section.

LIVE FOR CHRIST

Finally, the fourth discipline is one that will consume every day of our entire lives. We need to learn to live for Christ from the moment we wake up each day to the moment we fall asleep, to live in such a way that we draw attention to him and bring glory to him. We need to learn to live as Christians, to love as Christians, and to serve as Christians — to do all we do in a distinctly Christian way.

The heart of this book is investigating each one of these disciplines. If you are a new Christian, you will learn how to pursue godliness in a measured and balanced way. If you have been a Christian for a long time, you will take a look at your spiritual health and fitness, identify areas of strength and weakness, and make plans to grow all the more.

Through it all, I want to challenge you to make a lifelong habit of training yourself for godliness, and I want you to approach this training with purpose and order. After all, none of us have arrived. I don't think any of us would say we are as mature as we need to be, as we ought to be, and (I trust) as we want to be. An athlete can never stop training, and a Christian can never stop striving toward godliness.

ABOUT THE BOOK

I love words. In my mind, words represent the best kind of raw material. As a writer, I begin with an idea — information I mean to convey to others — and I labor to shape that raw material of words into a finished work that expresses the information with nuance, with freshness, with force. The degree to which I succeed is the degree to which I am satisfied with the result. It is a constant challenge and one I love to face.

I love words, but I also love images. Over the past few years, I have especially come to love and respect a certain kind of image — what we call infographics. Information graphics are a means of visualizing or displaying information, which makes it art, but an especially functional form of art. Visualization expert Alberto Cairo writes, "The first and main goal of any graphic and visualization is to be a tool for your eyes and brain to perceive what lies beyond their natural reach."[2] Infographics allow us to present information in fresh, powerful, and attractive ways — and in ways words cannot express.

This book began with a desire to learn and to teach how to live as Christians in this world. It combines the different passions of a writer and an artist — a writer with a passion for writing what is true and beautiful and good, and an artist with a passion for displaying what is true and beautiful and good.

This book is the product of our shared desire and our unique passions. It teaches the foundational disciplines of the Christian life through both words and illustrations. We want you to read the truth, but we also want you to see the truth. Our hope is that the graphics in this book will powerfully complement the words and that the words will powerfully complement the graphics. We want the truth to blend seamlessly through two very different media.

So come along. Join us as we describe — and display — the greatest of all truths.

SECTION ONE
GROW CLOSE TO CHRIST

CHAPTER ONE
GOSPEL

Recently, I walked into our church building, just like I do almost every day. I opened the office door and was greeted by the familiar screech of our alarm, warning me that I had thirty seconds to punch in my security code. I have entered the code hundreds and hundreds of times, but on that morning, my mind went mysteriously blank. I tried every code I could think of and got nowhere. By then, the alarm was blaring, the phone was ringing, and I was completely flustered. Even when the alarm company told me the code, I had no memory of it. It was the strangest experience. Somehow I had just plain forgotten an important piece of information that I use nearly every day.

We humans are a forgetful bunch. Our lives are busy; our brains run at full capacity; and sometimes it seems like for every fact we remember, there are one hundred we forget. Without help and without discipline, we are capable of forgetting even the most important information.

When we need to remember something, we usually embed it in a kind of habit or ritual. One of my hobbies is memorizing poetry. If I want to master and remember a poem, I need to repeat it to myself again and again until I can recite it perfectly. But that is not enough. I also need to develop a routine to continue reciting it to myself over the months and years that follow. The moment I stop repeating it is the moment I begin forgetting it. And this isn't only true when memorizing poetry. It is true in life, and it is true in our pursuit of Christ. The reason we celebrate Christmas and Easter is to provide the structure to ensure that we will regularly remind ourselves of the birth and death of Jesus. The reason we celebrate the Lord's Supper is to remind ourselves of what Christ has done and what he has promised to do. We are forgetful, so we develop habits and rituals to remind us of the most important facts.

There is nothing more important to the Christian than what the Bible refers to as the *gospel*, the good news of what Jesus Christ has accomplished. This good news is factual and historical, recounting real events that really happened in real places with real people. But this good news is also relational, a crucial component of this pursuit of growing close to Christ.

PURSUING CHRIST
THROUGH THE GOSPEL

One of the best parts of being a pastor is getting down — getting down on the floor with the little children and talking with them. They can't come up to my level, so I've got to get down to theirs. I often find myself sitting on the floor in my office having a chat with a few of them. I learn hilarious facts about my friends, details that have been filtered through the minds of their children. I also get to speak to the kids about their own hearts and souls. I trust this is good for the children, but I know it is good for me. It teaches me how to communicate important information in simple, clear ways. This practice pushes me to learn my facts even better, because if I don't understand something so I can communicate it simply, I probably don't understand it at all.

One of my favorite stories from the life of Jesus is told by his friend John. I love it because it displays the simple, childlike faith that God treasures. Jesus passes by a man who has been blind since birth, and Jesus' disciples ask him a simple but heartbreaking question: "Rabbi, who sinned, this man or his parents, that he was born blind?" (John 9:2). They assume this man's blindness is God's curse on him — either he or his parents must have done something terrible, and God has responded by cursing him with blindness. Jesus replies that neither is the case — God has made this man to be born blind so God could do a great miracle through him. Jesus then does something unusual and miraculous: He "spat on the ground and made mud with the saliva. Then he anointed the man's eyes with the mud and said to him, 'Go, wash in the pool of Siloam' (which means Sent). So he went and washed and came back seeing" (John 9:6 – 7).

The man is healed, but the story isn't over. The religious authorities hate Jesus and are driven mad with envy that he is able to perform miracles like this one. They refuse to believe that Jesus is actually responsible for this man's healing. Maybe it was all a trick, or maybe he isn't actually able to see. They call the man in and question him, demanding to know how his sight has been restored and who is responsible. He tells them it was Jesus, so they kick him out and question his parents instead. Still not liking what they hear, they bring the man in a second time and demand better answers: "Give glory to God. We know that this man is a sinner" (John 9:24). The man's response is simple and sublime: "Whether he is a sinner I do not know. One thing I do know, that

WHAT IS THE GOSPEL?

God sent his Son Jesus into the world in the power of the Spirit in order to live a perfect life, die a substitutionary death, and rise victorious from the grave (1 Corinthians 15:1–8). This gospel (or good news) is offered to everyone so that all who believe this message are saved from their sins (Romans 10:9–13). In response, Christians are to take the message of the gospel throughout the whole world, testifying to the glory and the grace of God (Matthew 24:14).

For further study, see:
The Gospel: How the Church Portrays the Beauty of Christ by Ray Ortlund

though I was blind, now I see" (John 9:25). This man does not know much, but he does know this: Earlier that day, he was blind, but now he has perfect sight. That is all he knows for sure, and that is enough.

Perhaps you can relate. For every Christian, there was a time when you were spiritually blind, unable to see the best and most important truths in the world. Then Christ saved you, and now you have the pleasure of sight. You see yourself as a sinner; you see Christ as your Savior; and you see the gospel as the good news that changes everything. The gospel is good news — *your* good news. And to draw close to Christ, you need to recount this good news and rehearse it again and again.

I want to pause to make an important distinction here. There is only one gospel — one real and saving gospel — but we can speak about it in at least two different ways. The gospel is objective and universal fact that is true for all people through all time. That is one way to speak of the gospel. But the gospel is also something every Christian experiences in a unique and personal way. In this sense, the gospel is both an announcement and an experience.

Each person who hears the gospel message is exposed to the facts at a different time, and each responds to them in a different way. We all have a gospel story to tell in which God swept into our lives and brought us his salvation. Before we go further, I want to start by considering the gospel in that second sense of personal experience and then return in a later chapter to the objective facts of the gospel. In this pursuit of growing close to Christ, I want you to ponder how you personally have experienced Christ's saving grace through the gospel.

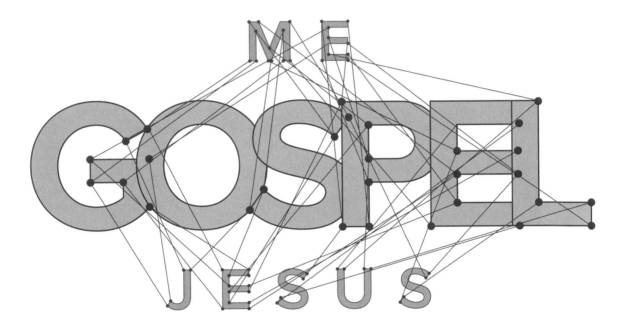

ME

GOSPEL

JESUS

THE RELATIONAL CONNECTION
BETWEEN ME & JESUS

RECOUNTING THE GOSPEL

August 8, 1998. For most people it was a day like any other, but for Aileen and me, it will always be especially memorable, because it was the day we were married. Every year, when August 8 rolls around, we pause to celebrate, and a sweet thing happens. When we sit and talk about that day, when we remember facing each other at the front of that church, and when we remember reciting our vows, we find our relationship growing and our love deepening. As the two of us sit on the couch and look at those old wedding photos, we inevitably find ourselves cuddling just a little closer. Recounting engenders intimacy. The experience draws us together, and our relationship grows through the simple act of remembering and sharing stories with each other.

This is the way God has made us — that as we remember together, we grow together. If we have a real and living relationship with Christ Jesus, it only stands to reason that it, too, will grow through the joy of recounting. We recount the gospel, and as we do, we grow in our relationship. There are specific ways we recount the gospel throughout our lives. We do this privately and publicly, formally and informally. Most importantly, we do it regularly and routinely.

PREACH

You recount the gospel when you recite it to yourself. Many Christians live with the sad delusion that the gospel is only the entranceway to the Christian life. They believe that the gospel gets you in, but then you need to advance to deeds, creeds, and meeting needs. But the good news never becomes old news. We never move past the gospel and never advance beyond it. Dane Ortlund writes, "The gospel is not only the gateway into the Christian life, but the pathway of the Christian life."[3]

The gospel is the relational connection between you and Jesus. It is the glue that bound you together and the glue that continues to bind you together. Aileen and I remember and recount our wedding ceremony and our wedding vows, and we wear our wedding rings to remind ourselves of our shared commitment to one another. As a Christian, you need to remember and recount the gospel to remind and assure yourself of your relationship with Jesus.

A WAY TO **SEE** MYSELF
AS A **SINNER**

THE **GOOD** NEWS

THE
GOSPEL

THE WAY FOR ME TO **SEE**
CHRIST AS MY **SAVIOR**

OBJECTIVE & UNIVERSAL
FOR ALL PEOPLE IN ALL TIMES

UNIQUE & PERSONAL

THE RELATIONAL
CONNECTION
BETWEEN ME & JESUS

THE CURE
FOR SPIRITUAL BLINDNESS

This habit is recounting not only the objective facts of the gospel, but the gospel as it pertains to you. It is one thing to say, "Humanity fell into sin and Christ died for sinful human beings," and quite another to say, "I am a sinner and Christ died for me." When you recite the gospel to yourself, you remind yourself of your own experience — how you were lost and how Christ found you. This makes the gospel intimately personal, a powerful experience shared between you and Christ. Recite the gospel to yourself, and you will grow closer to Christ. As C. J. Mahaney wrote, "Reminding ourselves of the gospel is the most important daily habit we can establish."[4] Do you remind yourself of the gospel every day? Do you recount the joy of your salvation?

EVANGELIZE

It is good and wise to regularly remind yourself of the gospel, but you also need to preach it to others. This is another way of growing in your relationship with Christ. In my marriage to Aileen, I don't just love her, but I also let others know that I love her. I tell people about my love for Aileen and the things I find lovely about her, and this honors her and brings me joy. One of the Christian's great joys is telling other people about Jesus. Not long ago, I spoke to a new Christian in our church who lamented a conversation with one of his clients. He said, "I didn't really get to tell her about the gospel. I only told her what Jesus had done in my family." I explained to him that he had done just fine.

Jesus once healed a man who had been oppressed by an entire horde of demons. After Jesus freed him, the man begged Jesus to be able to follow him, to travel as one of his disciples. But Jesus did not give his permission. Instead he told the man, "Return to your home, and declare how

THE LOCAL CHURCH

All believers are part of the universal body of Christ — the church (1 Corinthians 12:27 – 28). But God intends for Christians to join local expressions of his body (Titus 1:5) for the sake of fellowship, accountability, and spiritual growth (Hebrews 10:19 – 25). God calls his people to corporately enter his presence (Psalm 100:4), sing to him (Ephesians 5:19), and hear the Bible faithfully preached (2 Timothy 4:1 – 2). In order to preserve the unity and purity of the church, God gives elders to lead and shepherd the flock that Christ purchased with his blood (Acts 20:26 – 28).

For further study, see:
The Church: The Gospel Made Visible by Mark Dever

much God has done for you." Sure enough, "he went away, proclaiming throughout the whole city how much Jesus had done for him" (Luke 8:39). That same call is there for you — to declare what God has done for you through Christ Jesus. As you preach to others, you inevitably preach to yourself, once again recounting all that Christ has done for you and in you. Rarely are you given a deeper and clearer sense of Christ's love and presence than when you are declaring all the great things he has done in your heart and in your life.

WORSHIP

You also recount the gospel when you worship as part of a community of Christians, a local church. My love for my wife is strengthened as I hear others recognize the things I love about her and as they point out her many wonderful qualities. When they tell me about her, I think, *What a beautiful person she is!* We need other people to recount truth to us so that we do not grow narrow and selfish in our hearts. The Christian worship service is meant to be an ongoing reminder of the gospel. Worship services have traditionally followed deliberate patterns — a call to worship followed by confession of sin and assurance of pardon and a response of thanksgiving. Then there is the challenge that comes through the preaching and application of God's Word, and the benediction that serves as a kind of commission to a life of glorifying God by serving others. This kind of service mimics the structure of the gospel and encourages a congregation to join together in remembering and recounting the great truths of what Christ has done. This kind of worship is relational. As you worship God, you grow in your relationship because you are not just recounting facts about a distant deity, but you are experiencing his power and presence as well.

ORDINANCES

You recount the gospel when you celebrate God's special ordinances. God has given Christians two ordinances (sometimes called sacraments) that are designed to help them remember and recount the gospel and, by doing so, to grow close to Christ. Aileen and I celebrate anniversaries and birthdays together to recount our love. In a similar way, God gives us certain rituals, moments that mark our commitment and remind us of his love for us.

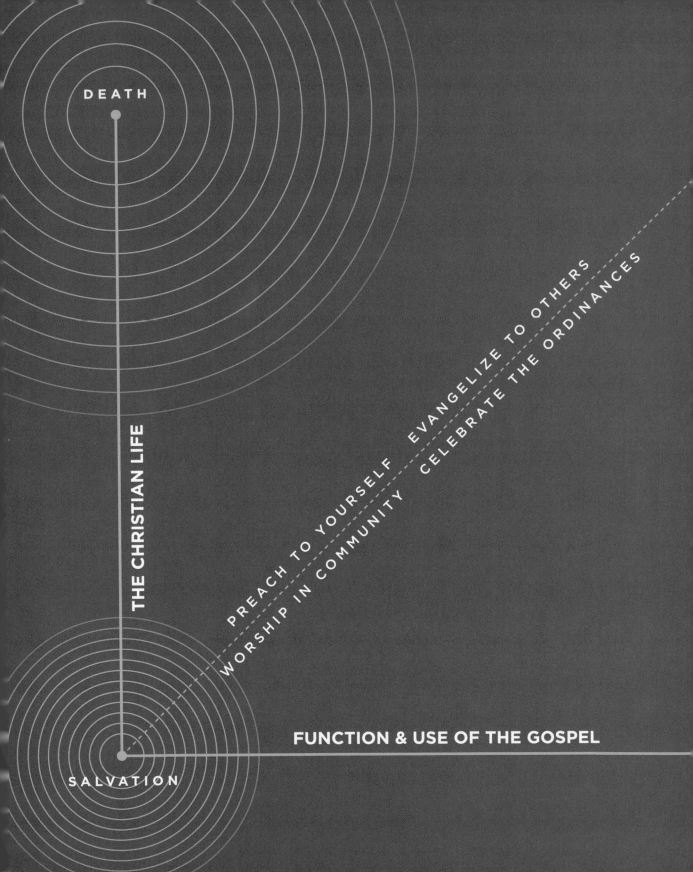

DEATH

THE CHRISTIAN LIFE

SALVATION

PREACH TO YOURSELF   EVANGELIZE TO OTHERS

WORSHIP IN COMMUNITY   CELEBRATE THE ORDINANCES

FUNCTION & USE OF THE GOSPEL

The first such ritual is baptism, and it is a beautiful picture of what Christ has done in your life. The water of baptism represents the washing away of sin, while going into the water and coming back out represents death and new life. God works through baptism to draw you closer to Christ. Wayne Grudem writes that baptism "is a sign of the believer's death and resurrection with Christ (see Rom. 6:2 – 5; Col. 2:12), and it seems fitting that the Holy Spirit would work through such a sign to increase our faith, to increase our experiential realization of death to the power and love of sin in our lives, and to increase our experience of the power of new resurrection life in Christ that we have as believers."[5] Baptism is not merely a symbolic act, but it is also a relational one.

The second ordinance, the Lord's Supper, is designed specifically to ensure that you regularly remember and recount the death of Jesus. When Jesus instituted this ordinance, "he took bread, and when he had given thanks, he broke it and gave it to them, saying, 'This is my body, which is given for you. Do this in remembrance of me'" (Luke 22:19). The breaking of bread is designed to remind you of the breaking of Christ's body; the pouring of wine is designed to remind you of the spilling of his blood. And through it all, you not only remember what Christ did, but you also grow in relationship with him as he is spiritually present with you in the celebration. As Dr. Grudem writes, "Today most Protestants would say, in addition to the fact that the bread and wine symbolize the body and blood of Christ, that Christ is also *spiritually present* in a special way as we partake of the bread and wine."[6] In the celebration, Christ is present, you are present, and your shared relationship grows.

CONCLUSION

Your pursuit of Christ begins with the gospel and continues with the gospel. As you believe the gospel, you come to understand that Christ has been pursuing you all along and that he has pursued you to the point of salvation. And now you joyfully respond and pursue him in return, growing in the sweet relationship you share with him.

CHAPTER TWO

IDENTITY

On February 6, 2006, Stephen Harper stood before the Governor General of Canada and recited the oath of office: "I, Stephen Harper, do solemnly and sincerely promise and swear that I will truly and faithfully, and to the best of my skill and knowledge, execute the powers and trust reposed in me as Prime Minister, so help me God."

In the very moment when he recited that oath, he received a new identity: Prime Minister of Canada. His new identity included what the oath calls "powers and trust": he received authority to represent Canada, power to make decisions on behalf of Canada, and responsibility to lead the nation in ways that are best for all Canadians. As a citizen of Canada, I want my Prime Minister to be constantly mindful of who he has become, to know what he is responsible for, to know what authority is his. I want him to take on the full identity of Prime Minister and to behave accordingly; if he will not take on that identity, he cannot do his job effectively.

I have never met the Prime Minister and have never been able to ask him, but it is my guess that taking on that new identity is difficult. Though he became Prime Minister in the moment he recited the oath, it must have taken him some time to begin confidently behaving like a Prime Minister. There must have been a period of adjustment when he was reconciling himself to all of these new realities — his new abilities, his new title, and his new leadership responsibilities. It must have been strange at first to hear people call him "Mr. Prime Minister" and always look to him for direction.

As a Christian, you also have received a new identity. Just as Stephen Harper was immediately given a new identity when he recited his oath of office, you were given a new identity in the very moment when you put your faith in Christ Jesus and became justified by him. It takes time and knowledge for you to grow into that new identity. All through the Christian life, you will be growing and straining to become who God has declared you to be.

As you attempt to live a spiritually healthy life and as you grow close to Christ, it is absolutely crucial that you understand who you have become and who you are. Let's look at just some of what is wrapped up in that new identity. We will do this under six headings.

I AM
IN CHRIST

Foundational to your new identity is this truth: You are in Christ. When I say you are in Christ, I mean you have been spiritually united to him so you identify with him and he identifies with you. There is a kind of inseparable union between the two of you.

My wife and I recently hiked in the Rocky Mountains, and far up a trail, we saw a massive redwood tree that had split near the base and crashed to the ground. Over time, the stump had begun to rot. As we looked at that stump, we saw that a new tree had taken root there and was now growing out of it. The two trees — the new and the old — had fused together so it was impossible to see where one tree ended and the other began.

Perhaps that can serve as a dim picture of what Christ did when he saved you. He once told his followers, "I am the vine; you are the branches" (John 15:5). That means you are like a branch that has been grafted onto a vine, becoming fused to the vine and utterly dependent on it for your life and health. In a mysterious and beautiful way, you and Christ have become one. Many Christians through the years have said that of all the blessings you receive as a Christian, none is greater than this. Why? Because it is only through your union with Christ that you gain all the benefits of Christ. Christ would be of no benefit to you if he had not united himself to you.

You should also know there are past, present, and future dimensions to this union. In the distant eternity past, you were loved by God and chosen in Christ to be an object of his love. God looked into the future, knew you would exist, and decided to bring you into a special relationship with Christ. Even then, he knew you would eventually have the right to share in all the benefits of what Christ would do. So Ephesians 1:4 can rightly declare, "He [the Father] chose us in him [Christ] before the foundation of the world, that we should be holy and blameless before him [the Father]."

1 Corinthians 15:22
For as in Adam all die, so also in Christ shall all be made alive.

Philippians 1:6
I am sure of this, that he who began a good work in you will bring it to completion at the day of Jesus Christ.

Romans 8:1
There is therefore now no condemnation for those who are in Christ Jesus.

I AM
IN CHRIST

I AM
JUSTIFIED

I AM
UNFINISHED

IDENTITY
IN CHRIST

John 1:12
But to all who did receive him, who believed in his name, he gave the right to become children of God...

I AM
FREE

I AM
ADOPTED

Romans 6:5-6
If we have been united with him in a death like his, we shall certainly be united with him in a resurrection like his. We know that our old self was crucified with him in order that the body of sin might be brought to nothing, so that we would no longer be enslaved to sin.

I AM
SECURE

Romans 8:38-39
I am sure that neither death nor life, nor angels nor rulers, nor things present nor things to come, nor powers, nor height nor depth, nor anything else in all creation, will be able to separate us from the love of God in Christ Jesus our Lord.

Then, two thousand years ago, when Christ lived on this earth, God looked at him and thought of you. Anything that Christ did as your representative, God counted as if you actually did it. God was considering you as belonging to Christ, as being one with his Son. In God's eyes, what Christ did, you did. When Christ lived a life of perfect love and obedience, God thought of you as living a life of perfect love and obedience. When Christ went to the cross to suffer and die, God counted your sins as belonging to Christ so that he suffered and died for you.

In fact, God even counted Christ's death as your death; he counted Christ's burial as your burial, Christ's resurrection as your resurrection, Christ's ascension to the Father's side as your ascension to the Father's side. And because you were united to Christ in all of this, all of Christ's blessings are now your blessings, and all of his benefits are now your benefits.[7] Romans 6 speaks of this reality at length: "If we have been united with him in a death like his, we shall certainly be united with him in a resurrection like his. We know that our old self was crucified with him in order that the body of sin might be brought to nothing, so that we would no longer be enslaved to sin" (Romans 6:5–6).

All of those benefits were stored up for you, just waiting for that moment when you would become a Christian and gain that new identity. Even in the future, you will forever remain united to him. First Corinthians 15:22 promises, "For as in Adam all die, so also in Christ shall all be made alive." You have been made spiritually alive because of your unity with Christ, and after death, you will be resurrected in Christ so that sweet unity will never end.

You are *in* Christ. He is your deepest identity. Whatever else is true of you, this will never change or waver: You are in Christ, and all that is his is yours. You can truly know him, so that not only do you know about Christ, but you are actually in relationship with him. Through this fellowship, this friendship, he brings you comfort and hope and assurance and peace. He teaches you and leads you.

I AM JUSTIFIED

Being *in* Christ is the foundation of our new identity and the means by which all God's blessings are ours. It is an incredible privilege, and one that is completely undeserved. And while it is inherently relational, it also has a legal aspect to it. You have also been justified by Christ. *Justified* is a term that comes from the world of law, from the courtroom.

If one of your neighbors robbed you, he would be in violation of the laws of the land. He would go to court and be found guilty. As a guilty criminal, he would need to be punished. This is why nations have penal systems — to enforce the law and punish the guilty. We all know that enforcing the law is crucial to the functioning of society. If we break the law, we are punished — and that is just and right. When your neighbor stole that money from you, he didn't just violate you; he also became guilty of violating the laws of the nation. It is fair and just that he would be punished by the authorities.

Just as you are responsible to obey the laws of the land as they are handed down by the government, you are responsible to obey the laws of the universe as they are handed down by God, its Creator and Governor. Every time you sin, you violate the law of the God who created you to live in perfect harmony with him and with everyone else he created. But you and I have failed to do this. We have sinned countless times, and this leaves us guilty before God — guilty of being a lawbreaker. And guilty people must be punished.

You are a lawbreaker, which means you are guilty before God and deserving of punishment. But as a Christian, you can be confident you will not be punished. Why? Because you have been *justified*. You have been declared innocent. And yet justice is still satisfied. How? Because Jesus Christ took your place, suffering the punishment your sins deserve. In the moment you trusted Christ for your salvation, God declared you were and always will be innocent and the full punishment for your sin has already been paid by Christ. God now thinks of your sin as being forgiven and of Christ's righteousness as belonging to you. He declares that you are fully righteous in his sight. It is as if you never sinned at all. Romans 8:1 expresses the glorious truth that "there is therefore now no condemnation for those who are in Christ Jesus."

When you belong to Christ, you are made right with God. There is no sin left to pay. There is not an ounce of guilt remaining. There is no sentence hanging over your head. There is nothing you need to do to be more accepted by God, and there is nothing you could do to be less accepted by God. You are forgiven, you are accepted, you are innocent, you are righteous, and you are justified. You can now relate to Christ as one who owes him nothing but your gratitude and service as you join into that glorious relationship.

So we have looked at two aspects of our identity so far. You are in Christ, you are justified, and now, as we will see, you are also adopted.

There are some things Christians do and say out of mere habit, but one thing Christians do that I love is calling other Christians "brothers" and "sisters." This isn't just a strange bit of formality. It is the application of a sweet truth. It is a reminder that when Christ saved you and me, he adopted us into his family. You are united to Christ, and through him you are now united to every other person who has ever been saved by him. We become a part of God's family with Jesus our elder brother and God our

THE TRINITY

God has revealed himself through his Word as one essence (or one being or one God — Deuteronomy 6:4) existing in three persons, expressed in the singular "name" of the Father, the Son, and the Holy Spirit (Matthew 28:19). From all eternity, God the Father has loved his Son (John 17:24) and, through the outpouring of the Holy Spirit (Romans 5:5), draws believers into that love (John 17:26). The Father chooses to save men from every nation of the earth (Ephesians 1:4; Revelation 5:9); the Son redeems them by his blood (Ephesians 1:7); and the Spirit seals their salvation (Ephesians 1:12 – 14) — all to display the glory of his grace (Romans 9:22 – 23).

For further study, see:
Delighting in the Trinity: An Introduction to the Christian Faith by Michael Reeves

Father. John 1:12 reads, "To all who did receive him, who believed in his name, he gave the right to become children of God."

As a Christian, you have been adopted by God into the one true family that spans the whole globe and the whole of human history. And there are some remarkable benefits that come with being part of this family.

First, being adopted by God means God is your Father. Galatians 3:26 tells us, "In Christ Jesus you are all sons of God, through faith." The God who is all-knowing and all-powerful and all-good and all-loving is your Father. Think about that: He is your Father! He is a good and kind and loving Father who cares for his children, loves his children, wants only the best for his children, and loves to relate to his children. You can cry out to him and praise him and trust him.

Being adopted means the Holy Spirit takes up residence within you. He assures you at the deepest level that God is your Father (Romans 8:15 – 16). He also leads you from within so you long for holiness and joyfully pursue conformity with God's desires for you. As the apostle Paul writes, "All who are led by the Spirit of God are sons of God" (Romans 8:14).

Being adopted means you can relate to other Christians as brothers, sisters, fathers, and mothers. It assures you that your relationships with other Christians are deep and meaningful — they are not distant acquaintances between strangers, but genuine friendships between members of the very same family. No wonder Christians love to join together in their weekly worship services. Each one is a family reunion!

Being adopted even brings you the privilege of discipline. At first, you may not think of discipline as a privilege. But as the author of the letter to the Hebrews reminds us, discipline is evidence of genuine love. "'The Lord disciplines the one he loves, and chastises every son whom he receives.' It is for discipline that you have to endure. God is treating you as sons. For what son is there whom his father does not discipline?" (Hebrews 12:6 – 7). God is a good Father who will discipline you when necessary, just like any good father disciplines his children for their own good. You may not like the discipline when it is being handed out, but a father who refuses to discipline his children really refuses to love them (Proverbs 13:24).

All of this is your privilege by adoption. As a Christian, you have been adopted by God. You are a child of God.

I AM SECURE

You are also secure. This means you do not need to agonize about your future or fret about God someday turning his back on you. You do not need to lie awake at night, tossing and turning and worrying about where you will spend eternity. Once you are in Christ, you will always be in Christ. You will never be separated from him. Those who have been justified will always remain justified. The innocent will never be judged guilty. The Holy Spirit will never abandon the one he has indwelled. Those who have been adopted will always be members of God's family. He does not cast out those he has drawn in. (See John 6:37; Romans 8:30; Philippians 1:6.)

Christian, you are absolutely secure. You can live your life free from fear.

You do not need to fear that God will grow tired of you, grow weary of your sin, or wish he had saved someone else, because he knew everything you would do long before he sent his Son to die for you. You do not need to fear hell, because you are promised heaven. You do not need to fear death, because you know that Christ has conquered death, and one day, you too will experience resurrection. You do not need to fear Satan, because Christ has triumphed over Satan. You can confidently believe the great words of Romans 8:38 – 39: "I am sure that neither death nor life, nor angels nor rulers, nor things present nor things to come, nor powers, nor height nor depth, nor anything else in all creation, will be able to separate us from the love of God in Christ Jesus our Lord."

You are secure in God's grip forevermore. There is nothing that ever could or ever will separate you from his love.

I AM
FREE

In all of this, you are free — truly and gloriously free. But you can only appreciate this freedom when you first understand your enslavement. Each of us is born into this world as a slave to sin, under the control of sinful desires (John 8:34).

Some live with a controlling fear of what others think, caring more about earning the approval of men than the approval of God. Some live under the control of addictive substances. Some become trapped in enduring patterns of sinful and selfish desires. And the Bible is clear that this world lies under the sway of our enemy, the devil, as well. Even when we are not bowing the knee to our own sinful desires, we may be bowing the knee to his. There are a million ways in which we are not free, especially in our own desires and decisions. Why? Because apart from Christ, we always seek what *we* want, not what God wants. We are all born into this world in bondage to sin.

Because you are in Christ, however, you have been freed to be like Christ. Because you are justified, you are freed from having to try to earn your salvation and from the crushing guilt of sin. Because you are adopted, you are freed to love your brothers and sisters far more than yourself. Because you are indwelled by the Spirit, you are freed from the power of sin — "He who is in you is greater than he who is in the world" (1 John 4:4). Because you are secure, you are freed from worrying about remaining in God's good books, freed from worrying that God will someday cast you off.

Christian, you are free. You are free from the dominion of Satan, free to worship and serve the God who has saved you. You are free to stop sinning — you have the power to overcome sin and to do those things that are good. You are truly and gloriously free.

I AM UNFINISHED

Finally, you are unfinished. This means you are a work in progress. Christ has saved you, and he has begun to have a relationship with you. Yet you still sin. You still return to those old ways at times. Too often, you delight to do what is evil. I do not know why God chose not to immediately and permanently eradicate every bit of sin and every desire to sin in the moment he saved you. But I do know he is committed to your holiness and that he will walk with you through all of life as you grow into this new identity, as you learn to be who you already are in Christ. Take heart. "I am sure of this, that he who began a good work in you will bring it to completion at the day of Jesus Christ" (Philippians 1:6). You are unfinished, but God himself is moving you toward completion.

CONCLUSION

It is impossible to overstate the importance of knowing your identity — who you are in relation to Christ. Your new identity makes all the difference. It changes everything as you live this Christian life. If you want to grow close to Christ, you need to know who you are and you need to know whose you are: You are in Christ, and you belong to Christ. There is no better person to be, and no better place to be.

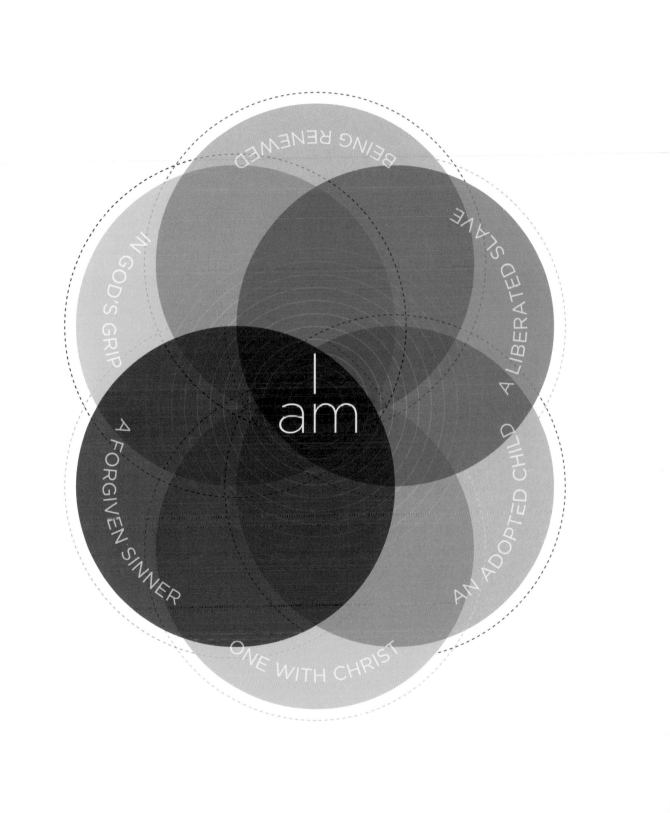

I am

IN GOD'S GRIP

BEING RENEWED

A LIBERATED SLAVE

A FORGIVEN SINNER

AN ADOPTED CHILD

ONE WITH CHRIST

CHAPTER THREE
RELATIONSHIP

We live today at the dawn of a great technological revolution. For several decades, we have been witnessing a worldwide explosion of digital technologies.[8] Have you ever considered how many of these new technologies are meant to help us communicate? Email is a modern form of postal mail; video chat enables us to extend face-to-face meetings to locations around the world; live-streaming provides the conference experience from afar; online relationships help us to maintain real-world friendships when we cannot be in the same place at the same time. We are relational beings, constantly inventing new ways to communicate with one another.

For a relationship to be genuine, it must be personal. It must involve interaction between two people. This is true of our peer relationships, and it is true of our relationship with God. As Christians, we have the privilege of having a genuine relationship with God in which he speaks to us so we can hear and understand him, and in which we speak to him in turn, trusting that he hears, that he understands, and that he responds. In general, we can say that we hear from God through the Bible, and we speak to God through prayer, but the two are more closely connected than that. As we read, we naturally pray, and as we pray, our minds focus on the truths revealed in Scripture. The more we commit to Bible reading and to prayer, the more of our lives we spend communing with God.

These two elements are the most basic disciplines of the Christian life — Christians are to read and pray — you know this. But though these are the basics, you will never master them and never grow beyond them. Throughout your entire life, you need to find greater joy in the Bible and deeper understanding of it; you need to find more joy in prayer and develop greater dedication to it. As a Christian, you need to be healthy here before you can be healthy anywhere else. In this chapter, we will consider how you hear from God and how he hears from you. In short, we will consider how God speaks and listens, and how you speak and listen in response.

HEARING FROM GOD

Every relationship is built on communication. It is impossible to be friends with a rock, because a rock doesn't have personality — you cannot communicate with it. You cannot have a relationship with the universe, because the universe is not a who but a what; it's a thing, not a person. But God is alive. And God is personal; he is a community of persons. Therefore, you can have a genuine relationship with him. Like every other relationship, this one is based on communication and the related practices of speaking and listening.

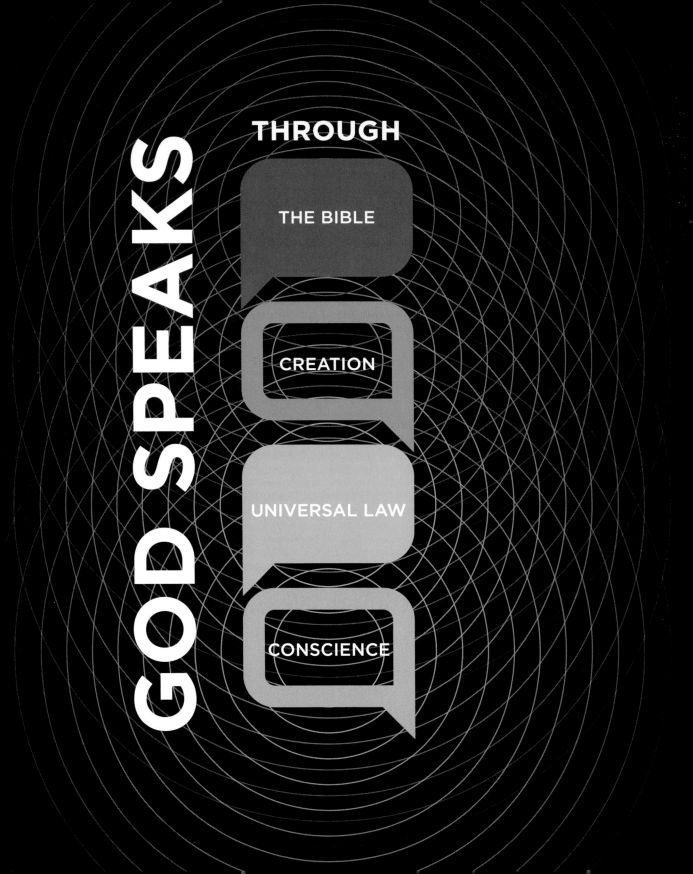

God wants to speak to you, and God *does* speak to you. First, God speaks to you and to everyone else through what he has created. The Bible tells us that "the heavens declare the glory of God, and the sky above proclaims his handiwork" (Psalm 19:1). All that God has created declares that he exists, that he is the Creator, and that he is glorious. God also speaks through our created consciences, which reminds us there are objective standards of right and wrong, of good and evil. The second chapter of Romans speaks of unbelievers who "show that the work of the law is written on their hearts, while their conscience also bears witness, and their conflicting thoughts accuse or even excuse them" (2:15 – 16).

While God speaks broadly to all humanity through his creation and through our consciences, he also speaks uniquely and personally, and he does this through the Bible. In the Bible, God speaks to us of his purposes and intentions and reveals to us things we cannot learn by looking at the world or listening to our consciences. Where creation and conscience provide general knowledge of God's existence and God's law, the Bible provides clear and specific communication about his nature and his plan.

A healthy Christian loves to hear from God through the Bible. He is constantly taking in God's Word — reading it alone, reading it with friends, reading it with family, reading it as it is woven into good books, hearing it read aloud in worship services, pondering it as he remembers it — consuming it in any way he can.

Let's look to the nature of the Bible and see why we need to dedicate ourselves to it. We will look at what the Bible is and then reflect on what it does.[9]

THE BIBLE IS A COLLECTION

We know the Bible as a book, a stack of printed pages stitched between two covers. Some today are learning to know the Bible as an app or electronic book, a collection of related information stored in various digital formats. But no matter how we engage the content of the Bible, it is an authoritative collection of works given by God to humanity. In days past, God spoke to and through certain people who wrote down God's own words (Hebrews 1:1). Some of these people wrote histories; some wrote wisdom literature or prophecies or

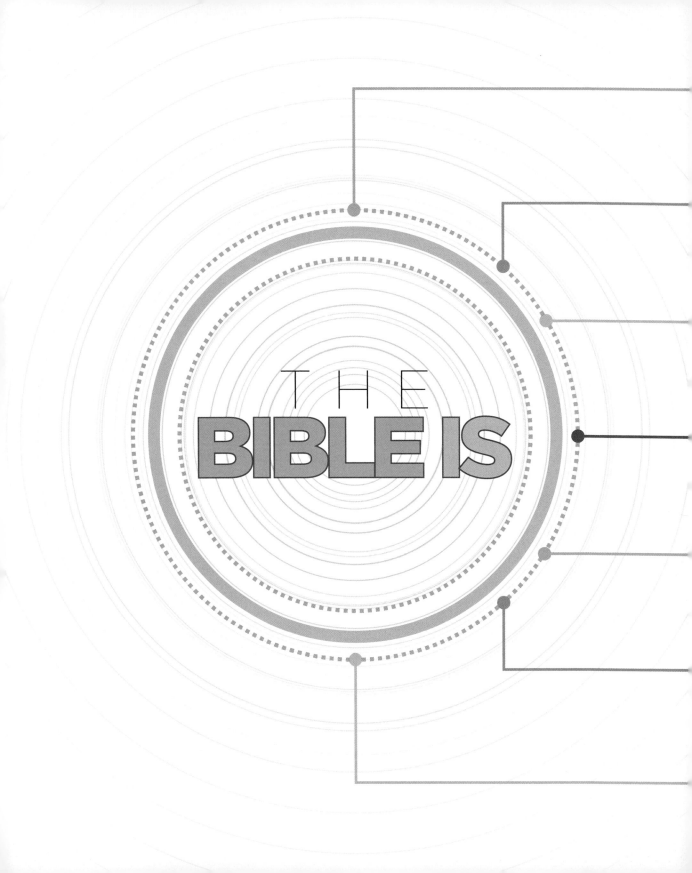

THE
BIBLE IS

A COLLECTION

The Bible is the authoritative collection of works given by God to humanity. The Bible, then, is what we call a canon, a complete and authoritative collection of one person's written works.

COMPOSED OF TWO TESTAMENTS

The most significant division in the Bible is the division between two Testaments, or two smaller collections of writing: The Old Testament and the New Testament.

A STORY

The complete collection of God's revelation to humanity is in the form of story—the story of what God is accomplishing in this world.

ABOUT JESUS

The focus and hero of the Bible is Jesus. In some way, every part of the Bible points forward to Christ or points back to him.

GOD'S WORD

God is present in and through the Bible in a special way so that he continues to speak to us today. His voice reaches out to us today through the Bible.

COMPLETE

God has spoken and given us the Bible, and there is no reason to believe that he will ever add to it. What he means to tell us he has told us.

TRUSTWORTHY

Because the Bible originates with God, it reflects the character of God. For that reason, we can believe that the Bible is without error and perfectly reliable. What God says is true.

letters. What they have in common — and what distinguishes them from every other bit of writing in the world — is that these words originated in the mind of God.

The Bible, then, is what we call a canon, a complete and authoritative collection of one person's written works. Each of these individual works we refer to as a book — the book of Genesis, the book of Isaiah, the book of Matthew, and so on. When we put the entire collection together, we call it a book as well — a book of books. Just as the giant *Complete Works of William Shakespeare* bequeathed to me by my grandparents contains a copy of each one of the plays penned by Shakespeare, the Bible contains a copy of each one of the books written by God.

THE BIBLE IS COMPOSED OF TWO TESTAMENTS

The most significant division in the Bible is the division between two smaller collections of writing — what we refer to as the Old Testament and the New Testament. The Old Testament extends from the creation of the world to a few hundred years before the birth of Jesus. The New Testament extends from immediately prior to the birth of Jesus to approximately seventy years after his death. In general, the thirty-nine books of the Old Testament point forward to the coming of Jesus, while the twenty-seven books of the New Testament tell of his coming and its significance.

THE BIBLE IS A STORY

The complete collection of God's revelation to humanity is in the form of *story* — the story of what God is accomplishing in this world. There is a unified theme that runs through the entire work and across all the different genres. The beginning and the end are related to one another by what happens in between. Each part of the Bible needs to be read in relation to the other parts. Gavin Ortlund says it well: "It should be read more like a novel than like the newspaper or a fortune cookie or a collection of Aesop's fables.

The whole thing hangs together, and the concrete parts are most meaningful when viewed in relation to the whole."[10] The Bible is a narrative that describes what God has done and is doing in this world.

THE BIBLE IS ABOUT JESUS

The Bible is a story, and the hero of the story is Jesus. In some way, every part of the Bible points forward to him or points back to him. Bryan Chapell writes that every text is predictive of the work of Christ, preparatory of the work of Christ, reflective of the work of Christ, and/or resultant of the work of Christ.[11] As the Bible tells the grand story of what God is doing in the world, it tells us how he is doing it through Jesus. Jesus is on every page of the Bible.

THE BIBLE IS GOD'S WORD

God is not silent. He has not left us alone without guidance in this world. Instead, he has communicated in the way we understand best — by words. Christians refer to the Bible as God's Word because it is full of God's words and because, when assembled, it represents his word, his message, to humanity. God wrote this message in a unique way. He used the words, thoughts, and creative abilities of people so they could pass on his divine message. Historians did research, gathered facts, and recorded their conclusions — doing it all in the power and with the guidance of the Holy Spirit. Poets observed, created, and wrote

INSPIRATION

God makes himself known to mankind through his Word, the Bible (1 Samuel 3:21). Since God's Word is truth, the Bible is without error (John 17:17). Likewise, it is inspired, or breathed out, by God (2 Timothy 3:16), since the Holy Spirit enabled men to speak and record prophetic utterances by directing their words within the context of their personalities and ministries (2 Peter 1:19 – 21). God intends to accomplish everything written in the Scriptures (Matthew 5:18) and will be successful in doing so, since his Word will never return to him empty (Isaiah 55:10 – 11) and cannot be broken (John 10:35).

For further study, see:
Taking God at His Word: Why the Bible Is Knowable, Necessary, and Enough, and What That Means for You and Me by Kevin DeYoung

under the guidance of the same Holy Spirit (2 Peter 1:21). And all of these were recorded as the Bible.

God continues to speak through the Bible today, opening the spiritual eyes of our hearts to hear and understand his Word as it brings conviction and calls us to respond to God in faith. We refer to this work as *illumination* — how the Holy Spirit helps us to understand and hear God as he speaks to us in the Bible. The Bible is unique among all the books in the world in that its words are "living and active, sharper than any two-edged sword" (Hebrews 4:12). God is present in and through the Bible in a special way so that he continues to speak to us through it today. This is why we can continue to refer to it as God's Word. His voice reaches out to us today through the Bible.

THE BIBLE IS COMPLETE

The Bible does not contain everything God has ever said or everything God will ever say. It does not contain the entire mind of God or a description of every act of God. However, we still believe that no information will ever be added to it. The Bible is complete in the sense that God has determined that his canon is closed. He has chosen to give no further revelation of that sort to us. The Bible contains everything God wishes for it to contain. God has said everything he needs to tell us to accomplish his purposes, especially his purposes in communicating the message of his salvation to us. We are never to add to it or take away from it.

THE BIBLE IS TRUSTWORTHY

Because the Bible originates with God, it reflects the character of God. For that reason we can believe that the Bible is without error and perfectly reliable. What God says is true. What God says he has done, he has actually done. What God says he will do, he will actually do. God is who he says he is, and we are who he says we are. Because the

Bible is reliable and trustworthy, we need to dedicate our lives to reading it, to understanding it, and to obeying it.

THE BIBLE DOES ...

The nature of the Bible tells us that we need to read and obey it. If the God who created the universe has spoken, it would be utterly foolish for us to ignore what he says. But if that is not reason enough, there are many other good reasons to commit to reading it and to living as if it is true.

Psalm 19 is a song of praise to God for giving us the Bible, and it's one of my absolute favorite parts of God's Word. At the time David wrote this song, the Bible was still in its infancy — only a small portion of the Old Testament had been given by God. But David still read it, pondered it, and praised God for it. In this psalm, he uses a series of words to describe the Bible, and then he praises God for the great blessings stored up for those who read and obey it. Here is what David writes in verses 7 – 11:

> *The law of the Lord is perfect,*
> *   reviving the soul;*
> *the testimony of the Lord is sure,*
> *   making wise the simple;*
> *the precepts of the Lord are right,*
> *   rejoicing the heart;*
> *the commandment of the Lord is pure,*
> *   enlightening the eyes;*
> *the fear of the Lord is clean,*
> *   enduring forever;*
> *the rules of the Lord are true,*
> *   and righteous altogether.*
> *More to be desired are they than gold,*
> *   even much fine gold;*
> *sweeter also than honey*
> *   and drippings of the honeycomb.*
> *Moreover, by them is your servant warned;*
> *   in keeping them there is great reward.*

THE BOOKS OF THE BIBLE

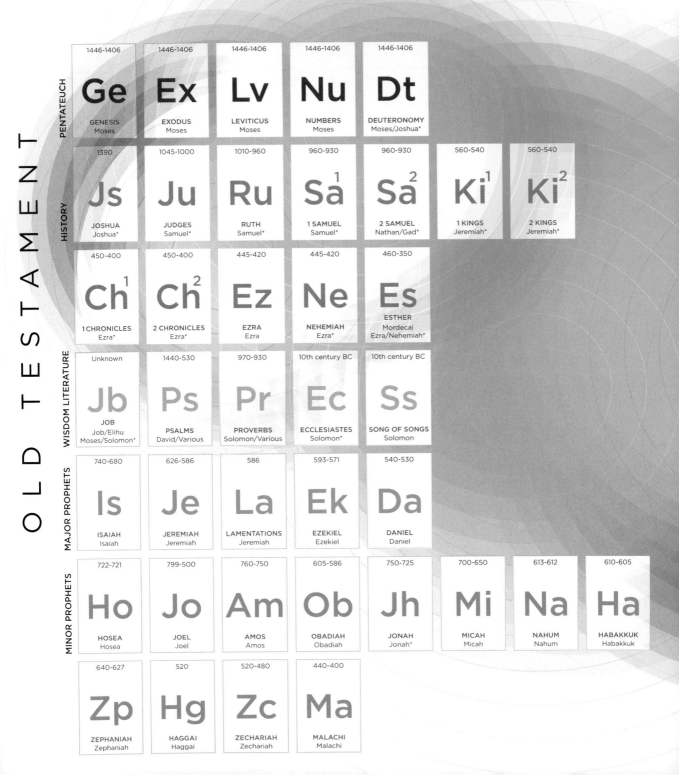

OLD TESTAMENT

PENTATEUCH

1446-1406	1446-1406	1446-1406	1446-1406	1446-1406
Ge	**Ex**	**Lv**	**Nu**	**Dt**
GENESIS Moses	EXODUS Moses	LEVITICUS Moses	NUMBERS Moses	DEUTERONOMY Moses/Joshua*

HISTORY

1390	1045-1000	1010-960	960-930	960-930	560-540	560-540
Js	**Ju**	**Ru**	**Sa**^{1}	**Sa**^{2}	**Ki**^{1}	**Ki**^{2}
JOSHUA Joshua*	JUDGES Samuel*	RUTH Samuel*	1 SAMUEL Samuel*	2 SAMUEL Nathan/Gad*	1 KINGS Jeremiah*	2 KINGS Jeremiah*

450-400	450-400	445-420	445-420	460-350
Ch^1	**Ch**^{2}	**Ez**	**Ne**	**Es**
1 CHRONICLES Ezra*	2 CHRONICLES Ezra*	EZRA Ezra	NEHEMIAH Ezra*	ESTHER Mordecai Ezra/Nehemiah*

WISDOM LITERATURE

Unknown	1440-530	970-930	10th century BC	10th century BC
Jb	**Ps**	**Pr**	**Ec**	**Ss**
JOB Job/Elihu Moses/Solomon*	PSALMS David/Various	PROVERBS Solomon/Various	ECCLESIASTES Solomon*	SONG OF SONGS Solomon

MAJOR PROPHETS

740-680	626-586	586	593-571	540-530
Is	**Je**	**La**	**Ek**	**Da**
ISAIAH Isaiah	JEREMIAH Jeremiah	LAMENTATIONS Jeremiah	EZEKIEL Ezekiel	DANIEL Daniel

MINOR PROPHETS

722-721	799-500	760-750	605-586	750-725	700-650	613-612	610-605
Ho	**Jo**	**Am**	**Ob**	**Jh**	**Mi**	**Na**	**Ha**
HOSEA Hosea	JOEL Joel	AMOS Amos	OBADIAH Obadiah	JONAH Jonah*	MICAH Micah	NAHUM Nahum	HABAKKUK Habakkuk

640-627	520	520-480	440-400
Zp	**Hg**	**Zc**	**Ma**
ZEPHANIAH Zephaniah	HAGGAI Haggai	ZECHARIAH Zechariah	MALACHI Malachi

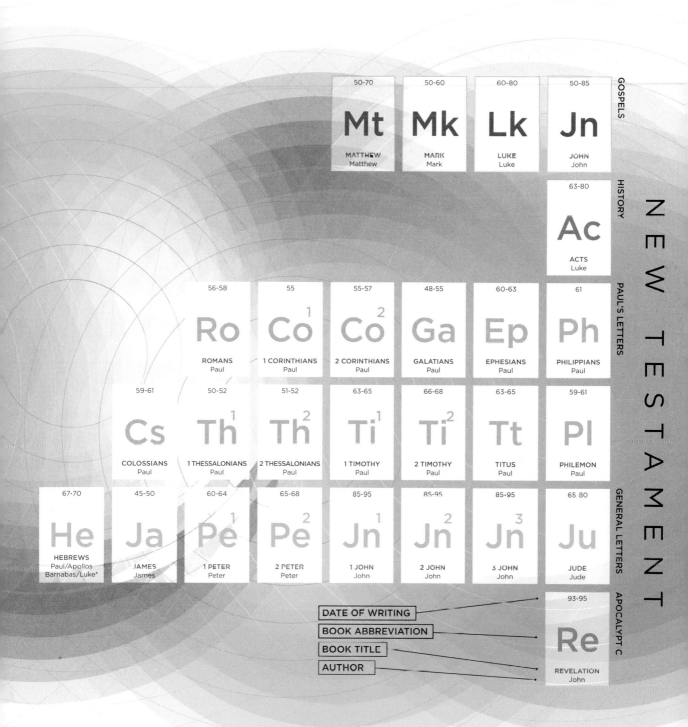

GOSPELS

50-70	50-60	60-80	50-85
Mt	**Mk**	**Lk**	**Jn**
MATTHEW Matthew	MARK Mark	LUKE Luke	JOHN John

HISTORY

63-80
Ac
ACTS Luke

PAUL'S LETTERS

56-58	55	55-57	48-55	60-63	61
Ro	**Co**^{1}	**Co**^{2}	**Ga**	**Ep**	**Ph**
ROMANS Paul	1 CORINTHIANS Paul	2 CORINTHIANS Paul	GALATIANS Paul	EPHESIANS Paul	PHILIPPIANS Paul

59-61	50-52	51-52	63-65	66-68	63-65	59-61
Cs	**Th**^{1}	**Th**^{2}	**Ti**^{1}	**Ti**^{2}	**Tt**	**Pl**
COLOSSIANS Paul	1 THESSALONIANS Paul	2 THESSALONIANS Paul	1 TIMOTHY Paul	2 TIMOTHY Paul	TITUS Paul	PHILEMON Paul

GENERAL LETTERS

67-70	45-50	60-64	65-68	85-95	85-95	85-95	65 80
He	**Ja**	**Pe**^{1}	**Pe**^{2}	**Jn**^{1}	**Jn**^{2}	**Jn**^{3}	**Ju**
HEBREWS Paul/Apollos Barnabas/Luke*	JAMES James	1 PETER Peter	2 PETER Peter	1 JOHN John	2 JOHN John	3 JOHN John	JUDE Jude

APOCALYPTIC

93-95
Re
REVELATION John

DATE OF WRITING
BOOK ABBREVIATION
BOOK TITLE
AUTHOR

NEW TESTAMENT

*Where there is a lack of consensus among evangelical scholars, we have listed the traditional author(s) for this book.

Let's look briefly at the six blessings God promises to those who read and obey his Word.

THE BIBLE MAKES YOU ALIVE

First and most foundationally, the Bible speaks about the state of your soul and promises to bring new life to it. David writes, "The law of the LORD is perfect, reviving the soul." The Bible brings about internal revival, and this revival is a coming alive, a conversion, of the whole person. God's unblemished Word stirs the dead soul to awaken it to eternal life. Ultimately, God works through his Word to save you from himself — from the wrath he must pour out on those who have rebelled against him.

THE BIBLE MAKES YOU WISE

"The testimony of the LORD is sure, making wise the simple." In the Bible, God tells you who he is and what he requires of you. This knowledge is sure and right, and as you encounter and believe it, it grows you in wisdom. If you want to be wise, if you want to see the world the way it actually is, if you want to see God as he actually is, if you want to see yourself as you actually are, you need to read God's Word.

THE BIBLE MAKES YOU JOYFUL

God's Word generates joy. David exclaims, "The precepts of the LORD are right, rejoicing the heart." The Bible gives you precepts — rules for your behavior and guidelines for your life. When you live in these ways, you live a life of joy, freed from your sin and freed to honor and obey God. You find that the greatest freedom does not come by following your own rules and your own way but by following God's.

THE BIBLE HELPS YOU SEE CLEARLY

"The commandment of the LORD is pure, enlightening the eyes." In the Bible, God gives you commandments — things you must do and things you must not do if you wish to honor and obey him. These commandments are not meant to be burdensome. Quite the opposite, these commandments enable you to see the world with clarity and to both please and honor God. We are often confused, divided in our desires. But when we place our faith in God and commit to him by submitting to his Word and obeying it, we grow in our ability to discern right from wrong, good from evil.

THE BIBLE MAKES YOU PURE

David is not finished yet: "The fear of the LORD is clean, enduring forever." God's Word is utterly pure, free from any trace of error or imperfection, and as you read it, you come to fear him. This is not the trembling fear of men before an evil and arbitrary dictator. It is the respectful and reverential fear of those who bow before an almighty God. God's pure Word cleans you, forever changing your thoughts, attitudes, and behaviors so you can live joyfully before him.

THE BIBLE MAKES YOU GODLY

David has one more: "The rules of the LORD are true, and righteous altogether." God's rules, his judgments, are true and absolutely unflawed. By reading the Bible, you can understand how and why God judges, and you can now live according to his standard; you can conform your life to his desires. To be godly is to be God-like in your character. The Bible enables you to live according to God's standards and to reflect his character.

WHAT THE **BIBLE DOES**

MAKES US ALIVE

The Bible brings about internal revival, and this revival is a coming alive, a conversion, of the whole person. God's unblemished Word stirs the dead soul to awaken it to eternal life.

HELPS US TO BE WISE

In the Bible, God tells us who he is and what he requires of us. This knowledge is sure and right, and as we encounter it and believe it, it makes us wise.

GIVES US JOY

The Bible gives us precepts—rules for our behavior, and guidelines for our lives. When we live in these ways, we live lives of joy freed from our sin and freed to honor and obey God.

GIVES US CLARITY

The commands of God are not burdensome but allow us to see the world with clarity and to both please and honor God.

HELPS US TO BE PURE

God's pure Word cleans us up, forever changing our thoughts, our attitudes, and our behaviors, so we can live joyfully before our God.

HELPS US TO BE GODLY

By reading the Bible, we can understand how and why God judges, and we can now live according to his standard—we can conform our lives to his desires.

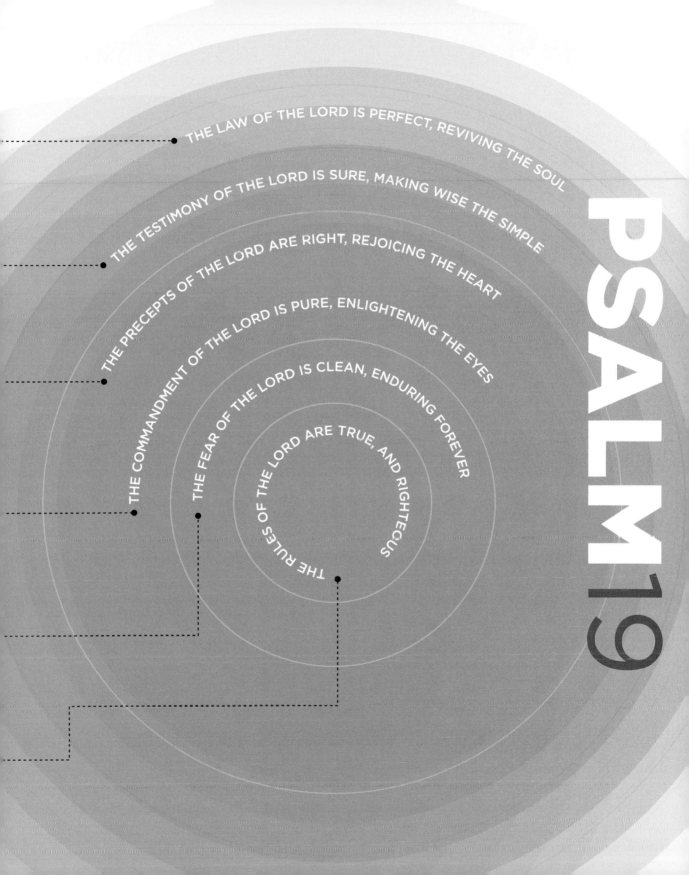

PSALM 19

THE LAW OF THE LORD IS PERFECT, REVIVING THE SOUL

THE TESTIMONY OF THE LORD IS SURE, MAKING WISE THE SIMPLE

THE PRECEPTS OF THE LORD ARE RIGHT, REJOICING THE HEART

THE COMMANDMENT OF THE LORD IS PURE, ENLIGHTENING THE EYES

THE FEAR OF THE LORD IS CLEAN, ENDURING FOREVER

THE RULES OF THE LORD ARE TRUE, AND RIGHTEOUS

No wonder, then, that David breaks out into a little benediction of praise:

> More to be desired are they than gold,
>   even much fine gold;
> sweeter also than honey
>   and drippings of the honeycomb.
> Moreover, by them is your servant warned;
>   in keeping them there is great reward.
>   — Psalm 19:10 – 11

If you will allow me the indulgence of alliteration, we see David praising God that the Bible is:

- **Precious.** Of all the earth's treasures, none — not even gold — is more valuable than the Bible.
- **Pleasurable.** David knew nothing that tasted sweeter than honey, but he still lauded the Bible as being far better.
- **Protective.** The Bible offers us the most important kind of protection — protection from the just wrath of God.
- **Profitable.** There are the greatest rewards associated with keeping and obeying God's Word.[12]

Ultimately, David loved the Bible because it was where he encountered God. He related to God through the Word of God because that is where he heard God's voice. You can do the same. As God speaks through the Bible, he makes you alive; he makes you wise; he gives you joy; he gives you clarity; he gives you purity; he makes you godly. Read it! Commit today, and every day, to reading and obeying the Bible. Love it and delight in it, just as David did.

SPEAKING TO GOD

There is another side of your relationship with God that we need to consider. Hearing from God is not enough. Relationships cannot thrive on one-way communication. It is difficult to conceive of a true friend who only speaks but never listens, who does all the talking without ever inviting you to speak as well.

I once read about a woman who decided her husband had been rude to her one time too many, and she determined to punish him by refusing to talk to him again. And she was true to her word. For several years, she was absolutely silent and did not speak a single word to her husband. Do you think that was a healthy marriage? Could their marriage relationship thrive under the silent treatment? Of course not. Relationships depend on two-way communication. And if you are to have a genuine relationship with God, this relationship will depend on listening *and* speaking. Prayer is the way you speak with God. It is a crucial part of a real, living relationship with God.

As you read the Bible, you will soon find that God expects you to pray. He expects it and even commands it. Just as we reflected on why you need to dedicate yourself to reading the Bible, we will look at prayer to consider what it is and what it does.

PRAYER IS ...

PRAYER IS RESPONSE

In all of life and salvation, God is the one who initiates, and you are responsible to re spond to his initiative. God took the initiative in creating you, and you need to respond to your Creator. God took the initiative in revealing himself to you, and you need to respond to his revelation in repentance and faith. God is the one who initiated a relationship with you by speaking out through nature and Scripture, and he expects that you will reciprocate the relationship through prayer. Prayer is not our initiation of a relationship, but our response. As Tim Keller writes, "Our prayers should arise out of immersion in the Scripture. We should 'plunge ourselves into the sea' of God's language, the Bible. We should listen, study, think, reflect, and ponder the Scriptures until there is an answering response in our hearts and minds."[13] Prayer and Scripture are not two separate ways to encounter God, but two dimensions of the same way.

PRAYER IS DUTY

God both expects and commands you to pray. If you acknowledge the existence of God and have a genuine relationship with God, of course you will want to obey him and do what he commands you to do. And he tells you to pray.

The New Testament is full of calls to prayer. Allow me to highlight just a few of them. As Jesus shares with his disciples what we call the Lord's Prayer, he does not begin by saying, "*If* you pray," but "*When* you pray" (Luke 11:2). He assumes prayer as a given for the Christian life. Luke 18 begins with these words: "And he told them a parable to the effect that they ought always to pray and not lose heart." There is an "oughtness" to prayer, a duty in it. Jesus himself, the sinless Son of God, often went out to quiet and private places to pray (see, for example, Mark 1:35; Luke 6:12). Paul in 1 Thessalonians gives the blunt command, "Pray without ceasing" (5:17). And in Acts 6, we see the early church calling certain men to pastoral ministry so they could dedicate themselves specifically to preaching the Bible and praying. It is the consistent testimony of the Bible: Prayer is a foundational practice of the Christian life, and it is impossible to imagine a healthy Christian who does not or will not pray.

PRAYER IS DELIGHT

Prayer is duty, but it is also delight, the natural overflow of the Christian's joy in the Lord. Parents who delight in their children love to spend time with them and speak to them. Wives who delight in their husbands love to spend time with them and to engage in conversation. Christians who love God find great delight in communing with him in prayer. As you spend time with God in prayer, you necessarily grow in your relationship with him, in your friendship. All relationships are built on the foundation of communication, and your relationship with God is no exception. When you and God converse through prayer, you grow closer to one another. Prayer at its best is a joyful outpouring of delight in a shared relationship.

PRAYER IS PEACEFUL ADORATION

Christians have long debated whether prayer is meant to be a time of quiet, contemplative adoration or whether prayer is meant to be a time to bring petitions and requests before God. But there is no tension here. Prayer is meant to be both. God means for prayer to be peaceful adoration, so that in prayer we quietly adore God and enjoy his presence in our hearts and lives.[14] Tim Keller says prayer "can lead regularly to personal encounter with God, which can be indeed a wondrous, mysterious, awe-filled experience."[15] Prayer is not an emptying of the mind and a resting in thoughtless silence, but a filling of the mind with the truth of God and a joyful communion with the God who is.

PRAYER IS ASSERTIVE SUPPLICATION

While prayer is not less than peaceful adoration, it certainly is more. The Bible tells us that we can go before God with our requests or supplications and expect that God will joyfully hear what we ask him.[16] The Bible tells us what we need and assures us that we can ask God to supply these needs. God tells us we should ask him with persistence, calling on him to do what he says he will do and to provide what he says he will provide. If even the unjust judges in this world will eventually give in to repeated demands for justice, how much more and how much sooner will God give good things to those who ask for them? (See Luke 18:1 – 8.)

Prayer is response, duty, delight, adoration, and supplication. It is all of those things and so much more. Prayer is one of God's greatest gifts to us and one of the greatest evidences of his mercy and kindness. Do you pray? Do you take hold of the gift? Now let's consider what prayer does.

PRAYER DOES ...

PRAYER BUILDS RELATIONSHIPS

The whole thrust of this section and chapter is this: Christianity offers a genuine relationship with the living God. I don't think I can say it too many times! Christianity promises that you can and will encounter the one true and living God. You can have a thriving and growing relationship with him. You can restore the relationship you were meant to have with him, which was disrupted by sin. You can enjoy this relationship for the rest of eternity. Prayer is an essential means of forming that relationship, fostering it, and increasing it. Pray to be close to God, and pray to remain close to God. Pray as a foretaste of the face-to-face relationship you will enjoy with him forever. Pray that you and God will be the best and closest of friends.

PRAYER

BRINGS RESULTS

God answers prayer. God is sovereign in this world and does whatever he wishes, but he chooses to act through prayer and because of prayer, not apart from prayer.

PEACEFUL ADORATION

Prayer is not an emptying of the mind and a resting in thoughtless silence, but a filling of the mind with the truth of God and a joyful communion with the God who is.

RESPONSE

In all of life, God initiates and we respond. God created us, and we respond to his creative work.

BUILDS RELATIONSHIPS

Pray to be close to God.

ASSERTIVE SUPPLICATION

God's Word tells us what we need and what we desire, and in prayer we ask God to supply them.

CHANGES YOU

As you seek him, and as you seek his will, he changes you to be more like him.

DUTY

God tells you to pray. If you acknowledge the existence of God and invite the presence of God in your life, you will want to do what he says.

PREPARES YOU

If God extends trial or difficulty, prayer will prepare us to receive it without despair and without anger.

DELIGHT

As you spend time with God in prayer, you necessarily grow in your relationship with him in your friendship.

PRAYER CHANGES YOU

One of the most common questions people ask about prayer is whether or not it changes God. "If God is unchangeable, and if he already knows the future, why should I bother praying?" This is a valid question with at least two sound answers. In the first place, prayer does not change the unchangeable God, yet it still does make a difference. God ordains not only the end of all things but the means as well. God ordains what he will do in a certain situation or to accomplish a certain purpose, yet he also ordains that prayer will be the means by which he does it. God acts through prayer, not apart from prayer. This means there are many things God will not do if you will not pray. But there are many things he will do if you will pray.

The second answer is that prayer is not meant to change God — to change who he is or to alter his eternal purposes. Prayer is meant to change *you*. As you seek God in prayer, your faith grows. God enables you to see his goodness, his grace, his glory, and even his purposes. As you seek him, you will find that you are the one who is transformed.

PRAYER PREPARES YOU

Because you pray, God will do certain things, grant certain things, or permit certain things he otherwise would not have apart from prayer. Prayer is one of the means he uses to prepare you to receive whatever he gives and whatever he does. If God extends great grace and mercy to you, prayer will prepare you to receive it without pride and without presumption. If God extends trial or difficulty to you, prayer will prepare you to receive it without anger and without despair. If God extends great means or great riches, prayer will prepare you to steward it faithfully instead of waste it foolishly. Prayer is like the trailblazer that goes out before you — it acknowledges your weakness and declares God's strength, and it prepares you, no matter the circumstance, to say, "God is good."

Because you are in a genuine friendship with God, he answers your prayers. At the most basic but astounding level, prayer works. It works! God is not obligated to anyone and does whatever he wishes, but he chooses to act through prayer and because of prayer, not apart from prayer. This means that prayer brings results. Prayer makes a difference to the world. Matthew 7:7 reads, "Ask, and it will be given to you; seek, and you will find; knock, and it will be opened to you."

It goes on: "For everyone who asks receives, and the one who seeks finds, and to the one who knocks it will be opened. Or which one of you, if his son asks him for bread, will give him a stone? Or if he asks for a fish, will give him a serpent? If you then, who are evil, know how to give good gifts to your children, how much more will your Father who is in heaven give good things to those who ask him!" (verses 8 – 11).

James 4:2 makes it perfectly clear: "You do not have, because you do not ask." It's that simple. You do not have the things you want because you do not ask for them. God has blessings stored up for those who will ask. Though God can act in any way he pleases, he chooses to work through prayer.

Prayer builds a relationship between you and your God; it changes and prepares you; and it just plain works. God uses this unique form of relationship to bring you countless blessings.

CONCLUSION

Never lose the joy and the wonder of knowing God and being known by God. You have entered into a relationship with the single most powerful and beautiful Being who exists. You have the joy and privilege of hearing from him and speaking to him. You are not merely the adherent of a religion, but a participant in a living relationship, a genuine friendship. So read to listen to God, and pray to speak to God, and grow in that most precious of relationships. Thank God for the immense privilege of being a friend of God.

CHAPTER FOUR

DRAMA

Have you ever read a really disappointing story? How do you know when you've come across an exceptionally bad one? It's a story full of shallow characters who develop inconsistently—or not at all. It's a story full of loose ends, of plotlines that begin and slowly fizzle out or just disappear altogether. There are few things more frustrating than getting to know characters and coming to care about them but then seeing them go nowhere. It is especially disappointing when a story begins with promise but then ends so badly.

But then there are really good stories. A good story flows beautifully from scene to scene. It introduces a character and develops him consistently and perfectly. It describes the tension between a hero and a villain and brings the story to a solid and satisfying conclusion. We know a bad story when we hear it, and we all love a good one.

The Bible tells us we are living within a great story, a great drama. In fact, it tells us this whole universe is a stage that exists to tell a story. You are one of the actors. In order to grow and mature in the Christian faith, you need to come to a sharper and deeper understanding of this drama—that you are part of something bigger, that something of cosmic, eternal importance is unfolding around you, through you, and in you. As a Christian, you are at your healthiest when you understand the fact that you are in a story and when you live with an awareness of your place within it.

THE WORLD IS A STAGE

There are many people who can admit the existence of a god, but who cannot tolerate the notion that he is intimately involved with all that goes on within this world. Some see God as the one who initiated the world's creation but then stepped back from it. Some see God as deliberately choosing not to know all that goes on in this world but instead learning with us and responding as best he can. The Bible teaches God's absolute sovereignty, his absolute ownership over this world and all that happens in it. God knows all that has happened, all that is happening, all that could happen, and all that will happen—he knows it all and in some way directs it all.

Why? Because God is up to something in this world. This world has a purpose, and everything in it exists to serve that purpose. Through all that is and all that occurs, God means to display something. The Bible is where he tells us what he is doing. Michael Horton says this well: "The Christian faith is, first and foremost, an unfolding *drama* …

This story that runs from Genesis to Revelation, centering on Christ, not only richly informs our mind; it captivates the heart and the imagination, animating and motivating our action in the world."[17] This world is a stage to display God's great drama.

If this world is a stage, there are many implications that make every bit of difference to your life and faith. Let's talk about four of them.

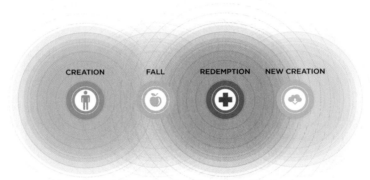

If there is a story, there is a storyteller. When events happen, whether good or bad, you do not need to look to fate or chance as if they are responsible. Instead, you can look to the storyteller to discover the purpose and meaning. You are familiar, I'm sure, with the great promise of Romans 8:28: "And we know that for those who love God all things work together for good, for those who are called according to his purpose." The promise that all things work together for our good can only have meaning if there is authorship, if someone is scripting and controlling this great story. It is a meaningless promise without an all-powerful God.

If there is a story, there is a hero. If there is a story and if you understand the way stories work, you know there must be a hero to this one. As you read it, you come to understand that you are not the hero of the story; Jesus is. The apostle Paul writes, "For by him all things were created, in heaven and on earth, visible and invisible, whether thrones or dominions or rulers or authorities — all things were created through him and for him" (Colossians 1:16). Everything in this world exists through Jesus and for Jesus, which means he is the great hero of this great story.

If there is a story, there is a plot. No story can exist without a plot, a story line that ties together the characters and the events. If there is a plot to this world, there is also a plot to your life. Your life is not meaningless. You are an actor in this story. You are making real decisions and taking significant actions. Through it all, you are playing a role in this great drama. And like any actor, you need to give yourself to that role more and more, so you can understand it better and play it better.

If there is a story, it is driving toward a conclusion. Finally, if history is unfolding in a deliberate and controlled way, you can be certain that what happens in the world is not just a series of isolated, disconnected, arbitrary events. Instead, there is a purpose moving forward toward a conclusion. This story never runs off-script. It continues deliberately and perfectly toward its satisfying closing scene.

There really is a grand drama unfolding around you. As a Christian, you have the privilege of understanding what it is all about; you can interpret what is happening; and you can see how you fit in.

THE GREAT DRAMA

This drama unfolds in four acts: creation, fall, redemption, and new creation. Everything that has happened and everything that will happen in history belong in one of these four acts.

CREATION

Creation is Act 1 of this story. The story line of this world began with a word. It began with a voice — the voice of the author — speaking into nothingness and saying, "Let there be light" (Genesis 1:3). God, the uncreated God who had existed for all eternity, spoke. With a word, he created light and separated it from darkness. And then, with more words, God created matter and time and places and things and beings. In six days, he created everything from nothing, and at the end of it all, he said it was very good (Genesis 1:31). It was perfect. There was not a single atom out of place, not a single flaw.

THE DRAMA OF GOD

IN FOUR ACTS

ACT 1
CREATION

GOD IS
THE CREATOR

In the beginning, God created the heavens and the earth.
Genesis 1:1

MAN WAS MADE
IN HIS IMAGE

Then God said, "Let us make man in our image, after our likeness."
Genesis 1:26

EVERYTHING WAS
GOOD

And God saw everything that he had made, and behold, it was very good.
Genesis 1:31

MAN WAS MADE
FOR PERFECT FELLOWSHIP

Know that the Lord, he is God! It is he who made us, and we are his; we are his people, and the sheep of his pasture.
Psalm 100:3

ACT 2 FALL

On the sixth day, God created something that was completely different from everything else he had made. He said, "Let us make man in our image, after our likeness" (Genesis 1:26). God took dust and formed it into a man and breathed life into him. This man was different from everything else God had created because he was made in God's image. Nothing else in all creation bore the image of God. From the man, Adam, God formed a woman, a wife, to help him, to be his companion.

The starting place was a garden. God created this man and woman and placed them in a garden, a place where God and man would dwell together, where God would walk and talk with them. God gave them everything they needed to live a perfect, blameless, God-glorifying life.

God created human beings to hold a special place in creation and to perform a special task: to rule over creation on God's behalf. In Genesis 1:28, God gave these people two big commands: First, "be fruitful and multiply and fill the earth and subdue it." They were to procreate, to create more humans, and to spread out to fill the whole earth, founding towns and cities and whole civilizations. And the second command was to "have dominion over the fish of the sea and over the birds of the heavens and over every living thing that moves on the earth." Humans were to have dominion over the earth and everything in it, to mine the earth, to use its natural resources, to tame the animals, to harness all that the world offers.

God gave humanity everything they needed and so much more. He held back just one thing: the knowledge of evil. Within the garden, God placed a tree called the tree of the knowledge of good and evil. And he instructed man not to eat of this tree. He could eat of every other tree in the world, and to do so would represent obedience and submission. But he could not eat of that one tree since that would represent disobedience and independence. The decision of the man would have cosmic consequences. As the first human being, Adam had been created to be a representative — the representative of all of humanity who would follow after him. His decisions would be binding on everyone who would follow in his lineage. Every person who would be born of Adam and Eve would inherit his submission or his rebellion — whichever he chose.

God created this world good — perfectly good. The act closes with these words: "And the man and his wife were both naked and were not ashamed" (Genesis 2:25). The world was so safe and so perfect that humanity could live naked and unafraid, naked and unashamed.

As the curtain rises on Act 2, Adam and his wife are in this garden and are living perfectly God-glorifying lives. They live in perfect harmony with one another and in perfect, unbroken relationship with God. It is paradise, a beautiful picture of the world as it is meant to be.

But it did not last. Satan in the guise of a serpent made his way into that garden (Genesis 3:1). He tested and tempted the two of them. He approached the woman and challenged her to doubt the goodness of God, to doubt the character of God. He challenged her with the thought that God had held back something that ought to be hers — complete knowledge rather than partial knowledge. God had told his people all about goodness but had withheld from them knowledge of evil. The serpent tempted Adam and his wife into believing they could be complete only if they also knew about evil (Genesis 3:4).

The man and woman fell for the serpent's lies. They doubted the goodness of God and determined to pursue knowledge of evil. They committed the very first sin by eating the forbidden fruit (Genesis 3:6). It was a simple act, but one that represented the greatest tyranny. They had decided to declare their independence from God. They had decided to raise themselves up in opposition to God.

They soon learned it was all a trick. They had been deceived. They suddenly realized that evil would not be out there, somewhere beyond them, but inside, welling up from within. Suddenly, they not only *knew* about evil, but they had *become* evil, darkened in their selfish thinking. The very moment they committed that sin, they plunged themselves and this whole world into that darkness. Their act introduced death and destruction and decay. We call this event "the fall" — humanity's terrible downfall from perfection into sinfulness.

Immediately, Adam and Eve recognized their nakedness and ran to hide and cover themselves (Genesis 3:7). Their shame over their physical nakedness symbolized the guilt they now felt under the all-knowing gaze of God. Man had rebelled against God and must now answer for his rebellion. The world had changed. The world had fallen. It

THE DRAMA OF GOD

IN FOUR ACTS

ACT 2
FALL

MAN FELL INTO SIN

...she took of its fruit and ate, and she also gave some to her husband who was with her, and he ate.
Genesis 3:6

MAN WAS BANISHED FROM
GOD'S PRESENCE

...therefore the Lord God sent him out from the garden of Eden...
Genesis 3:23

MAN'S RELATIONSHIP
FROM GOD WAS SEVERED

But your iniquities have made a separation between you and your God, and your sins have hidden his face from you so that he does not hear.
Isaiah 59:2

MAN AND THE EARTH
NOW LIVED UNDER A CURSE

Therefore a curse devours the earth, and its inhabitants suffer for their guilt;
Isaiah 24:6

ACT 3 REDEMPTION

THE DRAMA OF GOD

IN FOUR ACTS

ACT 3
REDEMPTION

GOD SENT JESUS
AS OUR REPRESENTATIVE

For our sake he made him to be sin who knew no sin, so that in him we might become the righteousness of God.
2 Corinthians 5:21

JESUS LIVED
A PERFECT LIFE

For we do not have a high priest who is unable to sympathize with our weaknesses, but one who in every respect has been tempted as we are, yet without sin.
Hebrews 4:15

JESUS DIED
AND ROSE FROM DEATH

That Christ died for our sins in accordance with the Scriptures, that he was buried, that he was raised on the third day.
1 Corinthians 15:3-4

WE ARE REDEEMED THROUGH
CHRIST'S BIRTH, DEATH, & RESURRECTION

In him we have redemption through his blood, the forgiveness of our trespasses, according to the riches of his grace.
Ephesians 1:7

ACT 4 NEW CREATION

was no longer a place of unbroken fellowship between God and man. It was a place of shattered fellowship. A grieving God drove man out of the garden, out of his presence. God and man were now separated, their relationship shattered (Genesis 3:24).

REDEMPTION

The curtain falls and rises again on Act 3. Man has fallen and is under God's curse. Even in the early history of humanity, we read, "The LORD saw that the wickedness of man was great in the earth, and that every intention of the thoughts of his heart was only evil continually" (Genesis 6:5). That is a horrifying indictment of human beings. It goes on: "And the LORD regretted that he had made man on the earth, and it grieved him to his heart" (Genesis 6:6).

God was grieved with man, but he was not done with man. God did not give up on humanity. Before God had even created the world, he had already set his love on some of those who would inhabit the world. God had a chosen people, and he continued to lavish love on those people, to pursue them even when they fled from him. The Old Testament is a long and grueling journey through the depravity of man as God's people turn away from him again and again, all the while finding new and creative ways to express their disgust toward him. God perseveres in his love, and he continues to call his people back to himself. He sends mediators to represent them, kings to lead them, judges to rule them, prophets to warn them. Finally, he sends his own Son. God becomes man to save man.

"God so loved the world, that he gave his only Son, that whoever believes in him should not perish but have eternal life" (John 3:16). Jesus Christ, the Son of God, took on flesh. He was born into this world as a human being so he could save human beings. He came into the world as the second great representative of humanity. As Adam represented us in his fall into sin, Christ would represent us in overcoming sin. He lived the life we fail to live and died the death we deserve to die. He went to the cross, where he faced God's wrath against sin, and rose from the dead in victory over sin. In all of this work, he represented us. He offers us the benefits of what he has done — complete forgiveness,

THE DRAMA OF GOD

IN FOUR ACTS

ACT 4
NEW CREATION

JESUS WILL
RETURN AND REIGN FOREVER

And the Lord God will give to him the throne of his father David, and he will reign over the house of Jacob forever, and of his kingdom there will be no end.
Luke 1:32-33

GOD WILL
BANISH SIN FOREVER

...as far as the east is from the west, so far does he remove our transgressions from us.
Psalm 103:12

MAN WILL BE IN
PERFECT FELLOWSHIP WITH GOD FOREVER

Therefore, if anyone is in Christ, he is a new creation. The old has passed away; behold, the new has come.
2 Corinthians 5:17

LIFE & RELATIONSHIPS
WILL BE AS GOD INTENDED FOREVER

He will wipe away every tear from their eyes, and death shall be no more, neither shall there be mourning, nor crying, nor pain anymore, for the former things have passed away.
Revelation 21:4

the gift of the Holy Spirit, and life that will never end—to all who will simply put their faith in him.

We live in this act today. We, as Christians, have been redeemed. We are calling on others to be redeemed. God makes it clear that this period of history, this act, will end only when all of his people have been gathered in, when all of his people have received their salvation.

NEW CREATION

We wait today for the curtain to fall on Act 3 and to rise on Act 4. The final act is "new creation," and it represents the future we are looking forward to with such great anticipation. It is the fulfillment and the perfect ending of God's plan—the final chapter that will go on and on and never end.

God promises that a day will come when he will put an end to everything that is evil. All evil will be taken away; all evildoers will be judged; every consequence of the fall will be reversed; there will be no more sin, no more sickness, no more pain, no more tears, no more sorrow (Revelation 21:4).

The greatest joy we experience today is just a taste, a hint, of what will be. Christ will begin an eternal reign, and we will be with him; we will reign with him. We will finally experience life as it was meant to be—an eternity of perfect and unbroken fellowship with God and man. The effects of sin will be reversed; the earth will be remade in complete wholeness and beauty; humanity will be perfectly joyful and perfectly fulfilled in God. We will finally realize and pursue the very purposes for which God created us in the first place. It will be everything we ever wished for and so much more. It will be goodness and joy beyond what we can even imagine.

This is the great drama the Bible reveals: a four-act drama of creation, fall, redemption, and new creation. All of history fits into these four acts, and every human being is an actor in it. God created the world so it could be the stage for this drama.

LIVING THE DRAMA

WHY DOES IT MATTER?

IT ANSWERS LIFE'S BIGGEST QUESTIONS

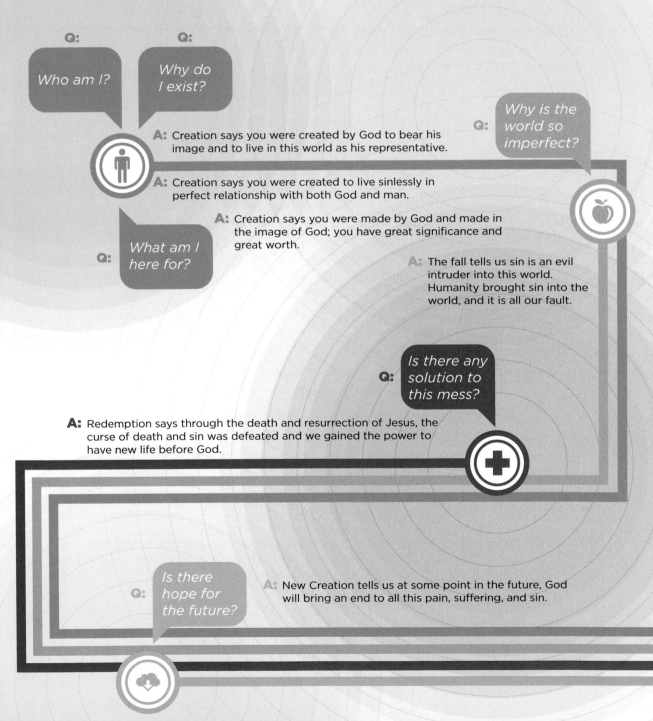

Q: Who am I?

Q: Why do I exist?

Q: Why is the world so imperfect?

A: Creation says you were created by God to bear his image and to live in this world as his representative.

A: Creation says you were created to live sinlessly in perfect relationship with both God and man.

Q: What am I here for?

A: Creation says you were made by God and made in the image of God; you have great significance and great worth.

A: The fall tells us sin is an evil intruder into this world. Humanity brought sin into the world, and it is all our fault.

Q: Is there any solution to this mess?

A: Redemption says through the death and resurrection of Jesus, the curse of death and sin was defeated and we gained the power to have new life before God.

Q: Is there hope for the future?

A: New Creation tells us at some point in the future, God will bring an end to all this pain, suffering, and sin.

LIVING THE DRAMA

I spend a fair bit of my life aboard airplanes. Every time I fly, I get to watch a small drama enacted before me. A flight attendant stands in the aisle with a little collection of equipment in her hands, and she demonstrates how to respond in the event of an emergency—how to unfasten a seatbelt, how to wear an oxygen mask, and how to inflate a life vest, in the unlikely event of a water landing. Like most passengers, I barely pay attention to these safety demonstrations because I assume I will never actually need to put any of that information into action. I assume it has no real bearing on my life, so I just carry on with reading my book.

You may be tempted to treat the dramatic story of this world in much the same way—as information that has little practical application to real life. But you would be dead wrong! This drama matters. Every day, there is immense practical value in remembering it, in knowing it well, and in growing in your understanding of how God's purposes are continuing to unfold in your life today.

CONCLUSION

Christian, if you want to grow in spiritual health, you need to come to a better and deeper understanding of this great drama. This drama is not something we impose on the Bible, but the big story the Bible imposes on us. It helps us to better understand the work of Christ and live like Christ.

CHAPTER FIVE

DOCTRINE

"Doctrine divides." I once heard a pastor say those very words. He was committed to keeping his church unified and working toward the goal of seeing souls saved. He was convinced the way to do this was to avoid doctrinal discussions of any sort. Doctrine, he believed, would open up rifts between the people of the church and cause them to veer off mission. Instead of longing to see souls saved, they would long to win arguments over the finest points of theology. Ironically, this church eventually lost its way like a ship whose anchor had broken away. The Puritan pastor Thomas Watson once wrote, "Knowledge of biblical doctrine is to the soul as an anchor to the ship, that holds it steady in the midst of the rolling waves of error, or the violent winds of persecution."[18] This church had no anchor, and at the smallest provocation, it drifted away.

I'm not entirely unsympathetic to the pastor's concern. Many Christians are, indeed, divided over doctrine. Too many congregations have been torn apart by petty disputes over the finest and least important distinctions. The pastor's concerns were genuine, but his solution was wrong. His church needed *more* doctrine, not less. That doctrine was critical to their mission. It would anchor it, motivate it, and lead to its accomplishment. Doctrine would help, not hinder.

Doctrine simply means "teaching." It is a word we use to speak of the facts, the statements of the historic beliefs of the Christian faith. Doctrine gives you the words you need to describe what you believe, and it will challenge you to live out the implications of this faith. Doctrine should be anything but dull and divisive. Doctrine should excite and unite. Doctrine focuses on the most amazing Being in the world and is meant to unite you to others as you strive together to be who he calls you to be. Doctrine represents the immense privilege God has given you — to know what is really true about him, about yourself and the rest of humanity, and about this world.

WHAT DOCTRINE DOES

This book is intended to be a visual introduction to Christian health, growth, and maturity. It is not, and cannot be, a thorough introduction to Christian doctrine. It would take many, many volumes to even scrape the surface of all that God has taught us. For now, though, we will consider six reasons every Christian ought to study and know doctrine — why you should learn the facts of who God is and how you are to live in his world as one of his people. I hope this section will provide the spark that will motivate you to read more, to dive deeper into the knowledge of our God, his Word, and his ways. To get you started, I have provided some suggestions for deeper study throughout this book.

DOCTRINE LEADS TO LOVE

Doctrine leads to love — love for God and love for others. When you study doctrine, you are really studying God himself, and to know God is to *love* him. Your love for God is limited by your knowledge of him. This means you can really only love God as far as you know him, and as the depth of your knowledge grows, so too do the depth of your love and your ability to live in ways that express that love.

But let's be careful here. Not *all* knowledge leads to love. After all, Satan, the great enemy of God, has been in God's presence and knows more facts about him than you and I do. And those facts cause him to hate God even more.

So you need to know facts about God, but you also need to assent to those facts. You need to believe that they are true of God and that they describe reality. But even that is not sufficient. You have to trust in God. You have to trust that this God is who he says he is, has done what he says he has done, and will do what he says he will do. Knowledge, assent, and trust — these three lead to an overflowing affection for God, affection that is fueled by the active presence of the Holy Spirit in your life.

And in this way, doctrine is not just a collection of dry facts, but rich truths that lead to greater love. When you know doctrine, when you believe doctrine as truth, it changes how you think and feel, and it leads you to prepare yourself to live in ways that express love to God. First John 4:8 makes it plain: "Anyone who does not love does not know God, because God is love." To know God includes knowing facts about God, but rightly understanding these truths enables us to enjoy him, to value him, to treasure him, and to act in ways that flow out of those affections. If you want to grow in your love for God and for others, study doctrine.

DOCTRINE LEADS TO HUMILITY

During the most recent Summer Olympics, I watched the strange sport of weightlifting, in part because I had recently started going to the gym and lifting weights myself. Yet while those athletes and I were both lifting weights, there is a world of difference between us. They lift exponentially more weight than I do. The difference between my abilities and their abilities puts my "strength" in perspective. I know my relative weakness when it is compared to their immense strength.

Perhaps this analogy gives you a small glimpse of what it is like to see God as he reveals himself. You begin to grasp the infinite distance between his power and your weakness, between his holiness and your sinfulness, between his unchangeable nature and your fickleness. As you see it, you are humbled. It is impossible to see God and to know yourself and still be a proud or arrogant person. The greater your knowledge of God, the greater your own humility.

Think of Philippians 2:3, where Paul exhorts, "Do nothing from selfish ambition or conceit, but in humility count others more significant than yourselves." Paul teaches you to cultivate humility by pointing you to the life and death of Jesus Christ. Growth in humility follows behind a true knowledge of God. And conversely, your arrogance is born from ignorance.

DOCTRINE LEADS TO OBEDIENCE

Just as you can only love God as far as you know God, you can only *obey* God as far as you know God. As you get to know God better, your affection and taste for God grow, affecting you at the deepest level and working itself out in your choices and decisions. When you do what you love because you love God, you are able to obey him from the heart. All throughout the Old Testament, God reminds his people of who he is and

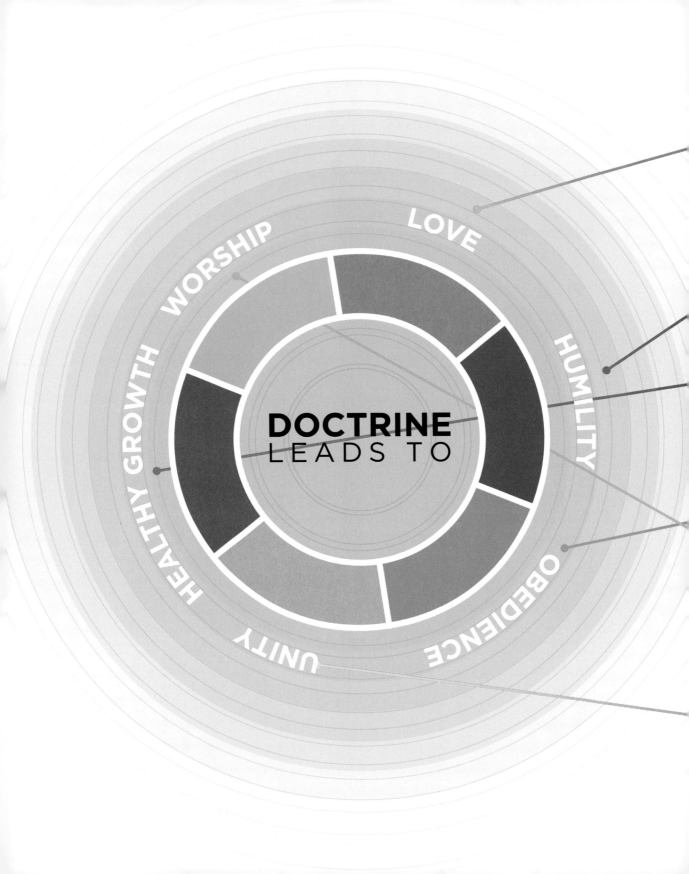

DOCTRINE
LEADS TO

LOVE

HUMILITY

OBEDIENCE

UNITY

HEALTHY GROWTH

WORSHIP

LOVE

Doctrine leads to love—love for God and love for others. When you study doctrine or theology, you are really studying God himself—and to know God is to love him. Your love for God is limited by your knowledge of him, so you can really only love him as far as you know him.

HUMILITY

As God reveals himself to you in the Bible, you necessarily see the infinite distance between his power and your weakness, between his holiness and your sinfulness, between his unchangeable nature and your fickleness. And as you see it, you must be humbled. It is impossible to see God and be proud. You cannot know God and be arrogant.

HEALTHY GROWTH

Doctrine protects the church and fosters her healthy growth. Every Christian who knows doctrine has the ability to rebuke anyone who contradicts truth and lead others in contradicting it. A church without doctrine and without people who know doctrine is a church that will be blown and swayed by every gust of wind.

OBEDIENCE

You can only obey God as far as you know God. As you get to know God better, as you get to know him more accurately, you are able to obey him better.

WORSHIP

Doctrine is meant to amaze you with the sheer power and magnitude of God. It will astonish you with the sheer sinfulness of mankind. It will bewilder you with your own insignificance before God and yet your sheer significance in his plan of redemption. The more you know of God, the greater your ability to worship God and the greater your desire to worship God.

UNITY

The shared truths about God bind Christians together in the truest and deepest kind of unity. There is a clear connection between doctrine and unity. There can be no unity in Christ without knowledge of Christ.

what he has done, and on that basis, he commands their obedience. When he gives them the Ten Commandments, he says: "I am the LORD your God, who brought you out of the land of Egypt, out of the house of slavery." It is only then that he commands their obedience, saying, "You shall have no other gods before me" (Exodus 20:2 – 3). By knowing God, they were prepared to obey God. By knowing God, his character, his works, and his ways, they should have had a deep longing to obey God.

In the New Testament, John links our knowledge and our obedience, writing, "Whoever says he abides in him ought to walk in the same way in which he walked" (1 John 2:6). What you learn of God and what you learn about yourself through the Bible must shape and mold your heart through the work of the Holy Spirit, equipping you to live a life that honors him. Doctrine is never meant to be a cold pursuit of facts, but a red-hot pursuit of the living God that leads to joyful obedience.

DOCTRINE LEADS TO UNITY

The shared truths about God that the church has passed down for nearly two thousand years bind Christians together in the truest and deepest kind of unity. In Ephesians 4, Paul writes about the way God gives leaders to churches "to equip the saints for the work of ministry, for building up the body of Christ, until we all attain to the unity of the faith and of the knowledge of the Son of God, to mature manhood, to the measure of the stature of the fullness of Christ, so that we may no longer be children,

THE APOSTLE PAUL

God dramatically saved (and renamed) Saul, the former blasphemer and persecutor of the church, to display his perfect patience and to proclaim his name (1 Timothy 1:12 – 16). Paul became the foremost missionary and church planter of the early church, and he had to endure an unusual amount of suffering so he might testify to the grace of God and preach the gospel to the Gentiles (Acts 9:15 – 16). His influence spread to many people, not only through his traveling and preaching ministry, but also through the letters he wrote, some of which are part of the New Testament (2 Peter 3:15 – 16).

For further study, see:
Paul, Apostle of God's Glory in Christ by Tom Schreiner

tossed to and fro by the waves and carried about by every wind of doctrine, by human cunning, by craftiness in deceitful schemes" (verses 12 – 14).

He draws a clear connection between doctrine and unity. There can be no unity in Christ without knowledge of Christ.

This unity extends to individuals in a local church, of course, but it also extends to Christians around the world. Yet it goes further still. It is a unity we share with believers in Christ — past, present, and future. It binds us together in a family that spans all nations, tribes, tongues, and times. Part of the joy of singing the great hymns of the faith together, and part of the blessing of reciting the classic Christian creeds together, is that we do so with a multitude of fellow Christians who are bound together in a common faith through a common Savior. Together, we are united by our knowledge of God as revealed in the person of Jesus Christ and in the Word of God, the Bible.

DOCTRINE LEADS TO WORSHIP

Doctrine is meant to amaze you as you encounter the sheer power and magnitude of God. It will astonish you with the awful sinfulness of mankind. It will humble you with your own insignificance apart from God and yet your sheer significance in his plan of redemption. It will move you with the incredible mercy of God as expressed in sending his Son to die for you and with the amazing grace of God as expressed in sending his Spirit to dwell within you. It will swell your heart with hope for Christ's coming return.

The more you know of God, the greater your ability to worship God and the greater your desire to worship God. What you learn of God should always motivate your worship. Knowledge of God warms your heart with affection for him and leads to deeper expression in your worship. It was at the end of his long theological reflection on God that Paul exclaimed in praise and wonder, "Oh, the depth of the riches and wisdom and knowledge of God! How unsearchable are his judgments and how inscrutable his ways!" (Romans 11:33). This was C. S. Lewis's experience as well:

I tend to find the doctrinal books often more helpful in devotion than the devotional books, and I rather suspect that the same experience may await many others. I believe that many who find that "nothing happens" when they sit down, or kneel down, to a book of devotion, would find that the heart sings unbidden while they are working their way through a tough bit of theology with a pipe in their teeth and a pencil in their hand.[19]

Indeed. Your worship of God grows both warmer and deeper in direct proportion to your knowledge of him.

DOCTRINE LEADS TO HEALTHY GROWTH

Finally, doctrine protects the church and fosters her healthy growth. In Titus 1, Paul looks to church leaders and writes that an elder "must hold firm to the trustworthy word as taught, so that he may be able to give instruction in sound doctrine and also to rebuke those who contradict it" (verse 9). To Timothy, he writes, "Keep a close watch on yourself and on the teaching. Persist in this, for by so doing you will save both yourself and your hearers" (1 Timothy 4:16).

While these calls go especially to church leaders, they continue by extension to all Christians. Every Christian who knows doctrine has the ability to rebuke anyone who contradicts truth and, even worse, leads others in contradicting it. A church without doctrine and without people who know doctrine is a church that will be blown and swayed by every gust of wind (Ephesians 4:14). It is your responsibility to learn doctrine so you can protect other Christians from error — and especially those Christians who are closest to you. Learn it and know it out of love for your brothers and sisters in Christ.

CONCLUSION

It is beyond the scope of this book to look at specific doctrines and to show how they promote love, humility, obedience, unity, worship, and healthy growth, though I have provided some examples in the study guide. Every doctrine is a gift of God, given for our good and his glory. Each doctrine gives you a sharper and clearer picture of the God who is and grants you the privilege of knowing him better. Christian, you are more than your doctrine, but not less. Sound doctrine is absolutely critical to the mature, growing, healthy Christian.

CHAPTER SIX

PUTTING OFF

We all have our heroes. We all have people we want to be like. One of the most startling realizations I came to as a father is that my son wants to be like me! He follows me; he watches me; he imitates me. Over time, I see my strengths reflected in him, and, far worse, I see my weaknesses reflected in him. I even see an imitation of my most annoying habits, like wandering in circles whenever I talk on the telephone. His youthful desire is Tim-likeness — a very natural desire for a son toward his father. Meanwhile, I can think back to my own childhood and remember all the ways I attempted to imitate my own father and to please him by being just like him.

God gives you both the responsibility and the desire to be like Christ — to be more like him than anyone else. Romans 8:29 assures you that this is exactly what God wants for you: "Those whom [God] foreknew, he also predestined to be conformed to the image of his Son." This is why God saved you — so you could be conformed to Christ's image, so you could imitate him and be like him. You need to be conformed to his image in your thoughts, in your emotions, in your intellect, in your behavior — in every way. You will want to see how he lived, and you will want to live like him. You will want to see what he valued, and you will want to value those things. You will want to see what he hated, and you will want to hate those things. You will want to see how he responded to life's events, and you will want to respond in the same way.

But be honest: You are a long, long way from your goal here. You think badly. You respond badly. You behave badly. You are a sinner. You are marred and marked by sin, so that Christlikeness seems so far away. How can you pursue it? How can you become like Christ?

Very broadly, the Bible lays out two ways you become like Christ: by stopping and by starting. You stop old habits, patterns, and passions, and you start new habits, patterns, and passions. The Bible uses a few metaphors to describe this process. Sometimes it uses the picture of clothing: You put off the old, sinful things and put on the new, righteous things just like you ditch your filthy work clothes to put on your church clothes. Other times, it talks about an old man and a new man — an old man who needs to be put to death and a new man who needs to be brought to life. Between the two pictures, they encompass a complete change in attitude, sentiment, and behavior.

In this chapter, we will focus on the first part of that — putting off the old man by killing old habits, patterns, and passions. Then, in the next chapter, we will shift our focus to the second part — putting on the new man, or beginning to act in righteous ways.

STOP PLAYING DEAD

John 11 tells the story of Jesus' good friend Lazarus. As this passage begins, we see a group of people coming to Jesus to tell him that Lazarus is sick and nearly dead. Jesus makes his way to his friend's hometown, but by the time he gets there, Lazarus has already died. Everyone is sad and mourning and quietly accusing Jesus. "You know, if only you had gotten here a little bit sooner, you could have saved him. After all, you are the miracle man" (my paraphrase of verse 21). But Jesus wasn't in a hurry because Jesus already knew how this story would end. He had something he needed to show everyone, and a lesson he needed to teach them.

> Then Jesus, deeply moved again, came to the tomb. It was a cave, and a stone lay against it. Jesus said, "Take away the stone." Martha, the sister of the dead man, said to him, "Lord, by this time there will be an odor, for he has been dead four days." Jesus said to her, "Did I not tell you that if you believed you would see the glory of God?" So they took away the stone. And Jesus lifted up his eyes and said, "Father, I thank you that you have heard me. I knew that you always hear me, but I said this on account of the people standing around, that they may believe that you sent me." When he had said these things, he cried out with a loud voice, "Lazarus, come out." The man who had died came out, his hands and feet bound with linen strips, and his face wrapped with a cloth. Jesus said to them, "Unbind him, and let him go." (verses 38 – 44)

In Lazarus, we see an amazing picture of what happened to you when you became a Christian. When Christ saved you, he brought you from death to life — spiritual death to spiritual life. Your heart and soul had been dead to God, lifeless and rotting. And suddenly God brought life, just like he brought life to the body of Lazarus.

When Jesus arrived, Lazarus had already been in that grave for four days. No wonder, then, that when Jesus told the people to open up the tomb, his sisters were concerned. The King James Version has them saying, "Lord, by this time he stinketh." Yes, he must have stinketh bad. He had been lying dead in a grave for four days in the Middle-Eastern heat. The unmistakable stench of death must have been all over him. We all know it: Dead men stink.

Then Jesus, deeply
moved again, came to
the tomb. It was a cave,
and a stone lay against it.
Jesus said, "Take away the
stone." Martha, the sister of the dead
man, said to him, "Lord, by this time
there will be an odor, for he has been dead
four days." Jesus said to her, "Did I not
tell you that if you believed you would see
the glory of God?" So they took away
the stone. And Jesus lifted up his eyes
and said, "Father, I thank you that
you have heard me. I knew that you
always hear me, but I said this on
account of the people standing
around, that they may believe
that you sent me." When he
had said these things, he cried
out with a loud voice,
"Lazarus, come out." The
man who had died came
out, his hands and feet
bound with linen strips,
and his face wrapped
with a cloth. Jesus
said to them,

"Unbind him. Let him go."

But let me ask, how long had your soul been in the grave when the Lord brought it to life? A lot more than four days. Was it fourteen years? Or forty years? It stank too. The stench of death was all over your soul. It was unmistakable.

Jesus called out to Lazarus and with a word brought life to this dead man. Lazarus came walking out of that tomb, wrapped in strips of linen like a mummy, and Jesus said, "Take off those grave clothes." People ran and started peeling them off. They took off the clothes that marked him as a dead man. Of course they did. It would be absurd to leave him wearing the clothes of a dead man when he was alive. Living people don't act like dead people, and dead people don't act like living people. It was time for this living man to behave like a living man. It was time for this living man to stop acting like a dead man. That was only appropriate. Lazarus needed to change his wardrobe.

And when God brought you to life, he told you to take off the sin that had marked you as a spiritually dead man or woman. You were clothed in your sinful thoughts, your sinful intentions, your sinful patterns, your sinful behaviors. You had literally done nothing good in your entire life — not one thing that was truly good in the sense of being done for the glory of God. But then God saved you and told you, "Now you need to take off those grave clothes." You need to take off those gross, smelly, dirty grave clothes and put on new, clean, beautiful clothing.

That's what you need to do when you talk about putting off the old, or when you talk about putting sin to death. You need to take off the sin that clings to you just like those grave clothes clung to Lazarus.

When you think about who you are and how you behave, let your mind picture those people unwrapping poor old Lazarus, taking off the clothes that marked him as a dead man. That is exactly what God calls you to do today and every day.

BE SANCTIFIED, BECOME SANCTIFIED

When God saved you, he immediately justified you. You were declared innocent. In the courtroom of God, you were declared to be innocent of all the sin you had committed and free from the just penalty that should have been yours.

Since Moses' day, God has called his people to love him with all their hearts (Deuteronomy 6:5). Jesus reinforced this great commandment (Matthew 22:37 – 38) and taught his disciples that the words of our mouths and the actions of our lives spring from the source of our hearts (Matthew 15:18 – 19). Giving honor to God with our lips is in vain if our hearts do not pursue him (Matthew 15:7 – 8). Therefore, Christians must guard their hearts with the utmost care and diligence (Proverbs 4:23).

For further study, see:

A Godward Heart: Treasuring the God Who Loves You by John Piper

But God was not finished with you in that moment. There is still the matter of sanctification — of growing in holiness. While you may wish that God would have immediately eradicated every little bit of sin, that he would have made it impossible for you to keep sinning, your experience is very different. You know you now have competing desires. You find you want to do what is right, but you also want to do what is wrong. You long to do what honors God, but there is a part of you that also longs to do whatever your selfish heart desires. You are caught in this lifelong battle between the old and the new.

Now there is a sense in which God actually did sanctify you in the moment you became a Christian (1 Corinthians 6:11). God now looks at you as holy. Though he sees your sin, he first sees your Savior and does not count your sin against you. And yet you still really and actually do sin. It's like you have walked out of the tomb, and the people have taken off your grave clothes, unwrapping you and setting you free. You take those first thankful steps toward Jesus but suddenly turn and run back to the tomb. You pick up those horrible, smelly grave clothes, and you wrap them around your body again. You run back into the tomb or jump back into the grave and begin to act like a dead man again.

And Jesus says, "No! I've set you free. You're alive. Act like you're alive, not like you're dead." And for the rest of your life, you are learning to stop acting like the dead man you were and to start acting like the living man you are, to stop thinking like the dead man you were and to start thinking like the living man you are. It's this constant battle to put all those old habits and patterns and behaviors aside and to embrace new ones.

In Colossians 3, Paul provides a whole list of behaviors that are associated with the old man. These are the kinds of things dead men do:

> Put to death therefore what is earthly in you: sexual immorality, impurity, passion, evil desire, and covetousness, which is idolatry. On account of these the wrath of God is coming. In these you too once walked, when you were living in them. But now you must put them all away: anger, wrath, malice, slander, and obscene talk from your mouth. Do not lie to one another, seeing that you have put off the old self with its practices and have put on the new self, which is being renewed in knowledge after the image of its creator. (verses 5–10)

Do you see the tension here? Paul says, "Here is a list of behaviors you need to put to death." And then he says, "You *used* to walk in these ways; you *used* to live in these ways. But *now* you need to put them to death." It's almost like he's gotten his timeline confused. But that's exactly the tension you live in. You have been freed from these things, but you keep going back to them. The power of these sins has been broken, but somehow you still allow them to dominate you. You have been given new affections, new desires, but somehow you ignore them and choose lesser desires and lesser affections. No wonder, then, that when Paul considers his own battling desires, he cries out, "Wretched man that I am! Who will deliver me from this body of death?" (Romans 7:24).

PUT SIN TO DEATH

Now let's get practical and talk about how you can actually put sin to death. That's what you want, isn't it? Aren't you ready to be free from those sins that cling to you like the soiled grave clothes of a dead man?

First, what is sin? It's a word we toss around a lot, but how do we define it? I don't think we can do much better than the *Westminster Shorter Catechism*: "Sin is any want of conformity unto, or transgression of, the law of God."[20] In other words, you sin when you do not conform to the rules that God gives you or when you just outright go against them. This is what you do when you sin—you deliberately transgress or break God's commands, or you just fail to live up to his full standards. Sometimes you outright disobey, and sometimes you just fail to deliver complete obedience. Sometimes you hate people, and sometimes you just don't love them as well as you should. Both of these are sin. As we said earlier, *sin is any failure to measure up to what God requires or any disobedience to his commands.*

How do you stop sinning? Paul tells you: "Put to death therefore what is earthly in you: sexual immorality, impurity, passion, evil desire, and covetousness, which is idolatry" (Colossians 3:5). How do you do that?

For many years now, the author John Owen has been my mentor in understanding the nature of sin and in discerning how to effectively wage war against it. Perhaps no Christian put more effort into the battle against sin than Owen did, and I would like to track with him as he describes a series of steps you can take to identify, understand, and overcome sin.[21] That may sound very official, but sin is deep-rooted and it takes deliberate effort to put it to death. You don't stumble or coast away from sin. Instead, you overcome it by carefully evaluating, identifying, and destroying it.

Consider a sin that is prevalent in your life, a sin you are aware of and long to destroy. Here is how Owen coaches you.

EVALUATE

Evaluate whether your sin is especially serious and deep-rooted. You have probably heard it said that all sin is the same and that no sin is more serious than another. There is a sense in which this is true, because every single sin has eternal consequences. But some sins have more serious consequences than others, and some sins are

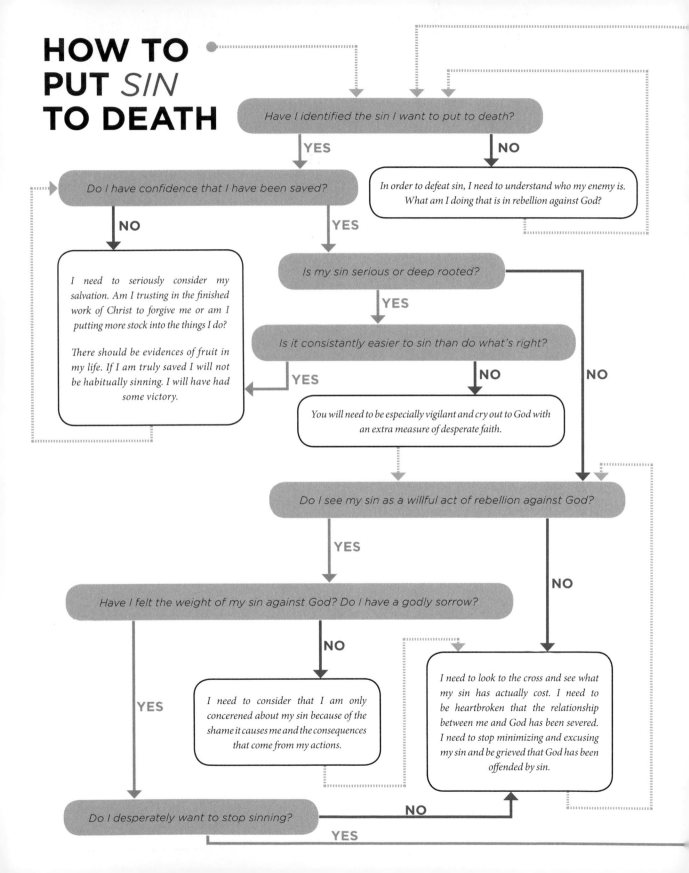

HOW TO PUT *SIN* TO DEATH

Have I identified the sin I want to put to death?

YES — **Do I have confidence that I have been saved?**

NO — In order to defeat sin, I need to understand who my enemy is. What am I doing that is in rebellion against God?

NO (from "Do I have confidence that I have been saved?") — I need to seriously consider my salvation. Am I trusting in the finished work of Christ to forgive me or am I putting more stock into the things I do?

There should be evidences of fruit in my life. If I am truly saved I will not be habitually sinning. I will have had some victory.

YES — **Is my sin serious or deep rooted?**

YES — **Is it consistantly easier to sin than do what's right?**

YES (leads to "I need to seriously consider my salvation...")

NO — You will need to be especially vigilant and cry out to God with an extra measure of desperate faith.

NO (from "Is my sin serious or deep rooted?") →

Do I see my sin as a willful act of rebellion against God?

YES — **Have I felt the weight of my sin against God? Do I have a godly sorrow?**

NO (from "Do I see my sin as a willful act of rebellion against God?") — I need to look to the cross and see what my sin has actually cost. I need to be heartbroken that the relationship between me and God has been severed. I need to stop minimizing and excusing my sin and be grieved that God has been offended by sin.

NO (from "Have I felt the weight of my sin against God?") — I need to consider that I am only concerened about my sin because of the shame it causes me and the consequences that come from my actions.

YES — **Do I desperately want to stop sinning?**

NO (leads to "I need to look to the cross...")

YES →

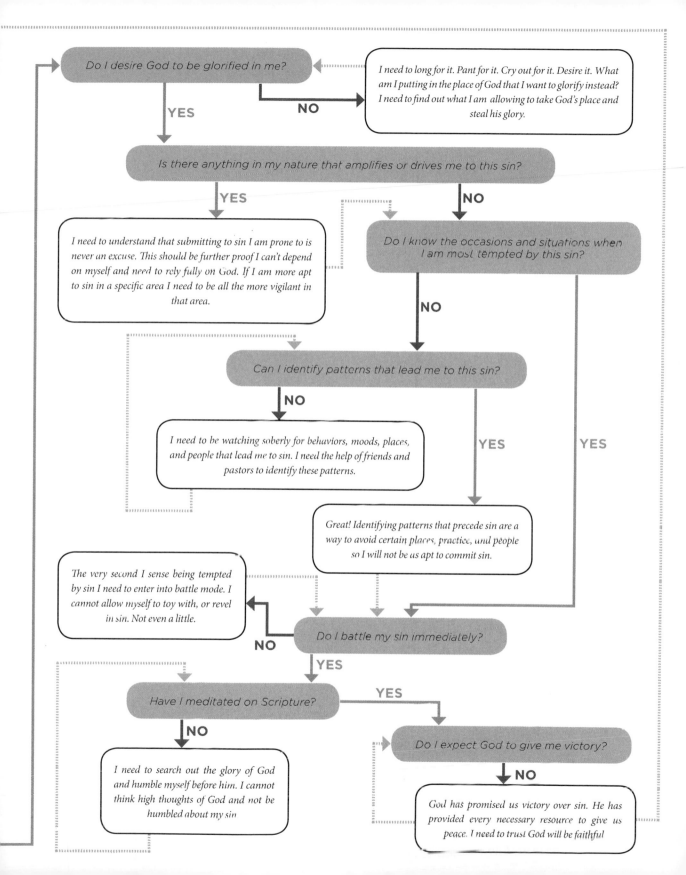

Do I desire God to be glorified in me?

NO → I need to long for it. Pant for it. Cry out for it. Desire it. What am I putting in the place of God that I want to glorify instead? I need to find out what I am allowing to take God's place and steal his glory.

YES

Is there anything in my nature that amplifies or drives me to this sin?

YES → I need to understand that submitting to sin I am prone to is never an excuse. This should be further proof I can't depend on myself and need to rely fully on God. If I am more apt to sin in a specific area I need to be all the more vigilant in that area.

NO → Do I know the occasions and situations when I am most tempted by this sin?

NO

Can I identify patterns that lead me to this sin?

NO → I need to be watching soberly for behaviors, moods, places, and people that lead me to sin. I need the help of friends and pastors to identify these patterns.

YES **YES**

Great! Identifying patterns that precede sin are a way to avoid certain places, practice, and people so I will not be as apt to commit sin.

The very second I sense being tempted by sin I need to enter into battle mode. I cannot allow myself to toy with, or revel in sin. Not even a little.

NO ← Do I battle my sin immediately?

YES

Have I meditated on Scripture?

YES → Do I expect God to give me victory?

NO → I need to search out the glory of God and humble myself before him. I cannot think high thoughts of God and not be humbled about my sin

NO → God has promised us victory over sin. He has provided every necessary resource to give us peace. I need to trust God will be faithful

punished more harshly than others (1 Timothy 5:24). The most serious sins are the ones that have gone deep enough that they are now habitual so your subconscious habits now lead you to sin again and again. As you consider your sin, you need to ask whether that sin is now manifested in your habits. Do you sin now almost on autopilot? Is it easier to sin now than to do what is right? If it is, your sin is especially deep, and you will need an extra measure of God's help to battle it and overcome it. If it is, you will need to cry out to God with an extra measure of desperate faith.

FILL

After you have identified the nature of your sin, you need to fill your mind and conscience with the guilt, the weight, and the evil of your sin. Let yourself see that sin in all its horror, to see that sin as an act of willful rebellion against God, to see that sin as an evidence of your deep sinfulness. Feel the weight of guilt. This step sounds mightily countercultural, doesn't it? All around you are calls to have high self-esteem, to forgive yourself, to move on. But you are far, far better served by allowing that sin to sit heavy in your conscience, by willingly grappling with your guilt.

Sin always tries to convince you that it is not very serious and that you do not need to be concerned about it. Sin says, "Relax. Others have sinned worse. This is just a little sin. You deserve this pleasure. You have done it before, and God didn't strike you down." You know how it works, I am sure. But you need to consider just how dangerous that sin is; you need to consider how it dishonors God, how it calls on God to discipline you, how it makes you less useful to the Lord's work, and how it may show that you are not even saved at all.

Look to the gospel, to the cross of Christ, not for forgiveness—not yet, though there will soon be time for that—but for the ultimate picture of the cost of your sin as Christ suffers and dies for that sin you want to commit. Consider how patient and kind God has been with you in allowing you to go on without striking you down for your sin. Consider all the ways he has been gracious to you from the moment of your birth until today. Feel all of that. Feel the weight, the guilt, of it. See Christ bearing your sin on the cross, and do not avert your gaze until that view sits heavy in your soul.

Heath Lambert offers counsel at just this point and calls you to godly sorrow, which "may look just as sad as the worldly variety, but something very different is happening in the heart. Worldly sorrow is sad over losing the things of the world, while the focus of godly sorrow is God himself. Godly sorrow is pained over the break in relationship with God. It is heartbroken that God has been grieved and offended. The tears of godly sorrow flow from the sadness that God's loving and holy law has been broken."[22]

Weep those tears of godly sorrow.

LONG

You have evaluated the sin, filled your mind and soul with the evil of it, and loaded your conscience with the guilt of it. Christian, you must now be longing for deliverance from that sin. Don't you want to be free from it? You now see your sin in sharp focus, and that sin looks horrible. Now, and only now, you are in the right place to long for deliverance from it. Now you want to put that sin to death for the best reasons. You are not simply caught up in the fear of consequences or the fear of shame and embarrassment. No, now you see the cost and guilt of your sin, and you long to be delivered from it so God can be glorified in you. Long for it. Pant for it. Cry out for it. Desire to be free from it. And take heart, "the power of God melts despair when you grasp his forgiving and transforming grace through repentance."[23]

CONSIDER

Pause here for a moment to consider whether there are ways this sin is amplified by your nature or your natural disposition. Is there something in your life, your history, or even your family history that makes you especially prone to this sin? Some people seem to come from families of alcoholics, and it may be there is some predisposition to addiction within them. Some people have melancholy personalities that may make them prone to grumbling or very excitable personalities that make them prone to great outbursts of anger. Or perhaps someone sinned against you earlier in life, and the shame over what happened leads you to act out in sinful ways.

All of these things may be true, and they may indicate a kind of proneness or predisposition to sin. But they never provide an excuse. Where you are prone to sin because of your nature or background, allow this disposition to further convince you of your weakness and your desperate need for God's strength. If you are predisposed toward a sin, it doesn't in the least excuse you for falling into it; instead, it puts the burden on you to fight even harder against it, to destroy it completely, and to be especially vigilant in watching for it to reappear.

CONTEMPLATE

It is time to take action against that sin. As you put together a plan, you need to contemplate the occasions in which this sin breaks out. When a sin is particularly stubborn and you are particularly prone to it, you will inevitably find you have developed patterns that lead you to the sin. So think about the times when you tend to fall into this sin. What are the occasions surrounding it? What events happen right before it? What are the habits or patterns that lead to it? What mood or frame of mind tends to precede it? Think about these things; develop an awareness of your habits, patterns, and behaviors before you actually commit the sin; and stop the downward spiral long before it gets to the point of sinning. You rarely commit a big sin without first sliding down a long and slippery slope of little sins. So consider those little sins, and identify the patterns.

Also contemplate where you need to take radical action against your sin. When Jesus spoke about deep-rooted sin, he called his followers to be willing to take extreme measures. "If your right eye causes you to sin, tear it out and throw it away. For it is better that you lose one of your members than that your whole body be thrown into hell. And if your right hand causes you to sin, cut it off and throw it away. For it is better that you lose one of your members than that your whole body go into hell" (Matthew 5:29 – 30). Was Jesus actually calling for self-mutilation? No, because it is your *heart*, not your body, that is the root of sin. Instead, he was calling you to deal with your sin with the utmost seriousness.

BATTLE

Now commit to battling hard against the very first awakenings of that sin. Never, ever allow yourself to toy with sin. Never think you will sin only this far, but no further. The very second you feel that sin awakening within you, determine you will not succumb to it. Cry out to God in that very moment. He lives within you through the Holy Spirit, so he is always close, and his power is always available. Call for his help. And call for help from other Christians as well. God has put us in community with other Christians so we can strengthen and encourage one another.

Sin is like water held back by a dam. The moment there is even a small crack in that dam, the weight of the water pushing against it will blow a hole right through, and the entire structure will collapse. Do not think you can control your sin and allow only so much of it. If you do that, sin will win every time. Thomas Brooks says it well: "A little hole in the ship sinks it; a small breach in a sea-bank carries away all before it; a little stab at the heart kills a man; and a little sin, without a great deal of mercy, will damn a man."[24]

MEDITATE

As the desire to sin rises up and as you commit yourself to battling against it, meditate on God to see his glory and your desperate inability. Think about God. Read his Word and meditate on it. Especially search out the glory of God and think about the massive distance between you and him. Think of how great he is and how little you know of him. Humble yourself by thinking great thoughts of God. God promises that he opposes the proud but gives grace to the humble (James 4:6; 1 Peter 5:5); if you want his grace in battling sin, you need to humble yourself by considering God and by meeting with God (James 4:8). You can't think high thoughts of God and not be overwhelmed by sorrow for sin.

I have always appreciated R. C. Sproul's grappling with the glory and holiness of God:

> It's dangerous to assume that because a person is drawn to holiness in his study that he is thereby a holy man. There is irony here. I am sure that the reason I have a deep hunger to learn of the holiness of God is precisely because I am not holy. I am a profane man — a man who spends more time out of the temple than in it. But I have had just enough of a taste of the majesty of God to want more. I know what it means to be a forgiven man and what it means to be sent on a mission. My soul cries for more. My soul needs more.[25]

If you meditate on the holiness of God, you will long to be holy even as he is holy (1 Peter 1:14 – 16).

EXPECT

Finally, expect to hear God speak peace to your soul. As you do all of these things and follow each of these steps, you can expect that God will help you put your sin to death and will give you peace in your mind and conscience. You will *feel peace* because you will be *at peace*. No matter how eager you are to see this sin put to death, you can be sure that God is even more eager. No matter how great an offense it is to you, it is a much greater offense to him.

There is one important thing you must guard against: Do not speak peace to yourself until God does. You may be tempted to see your desire to put the sin to death as actually putting the sin to death. Or you may be too quick to think you have been completely cured of that sin. Be very, very careful. It is God who has the right to speak freedom and peace to your conscience, to your heart, to your mind. Let God speak it through his Spirit, through his Word, and through his people. When he does, listen. But don't speak it to yourself too soon, or you will be deluding yourself and will go straight back into your sin. Listen for God's affirming voice and look for success. God is for you, and he loves to help you put your sin to death. It is his delight.

CONCLUSION

Christian, you are alive. You have been made alive by God and have the ability to act like it. Stop running back to the grave. Stay with Jesus, abide in Jesus, and put your sin to death today and every day. Apply yourself to the daily battle against sin and expect that God will meet you in that battle. Expect that he will lead you to victory. As much as you hate your sin, you can be certain that God hates it far more. No matter how committed you are to putting that sin to death, you can be certain that God is even more committed.

PUTTING SIN TO DEATH

- **EVALUATE**
Is your sin especially serious and deep-rooted?

- **FILL**
Immerse your mind and conscience with the guilt, the weight, and the evil of your sin.

- **CONSIDER**
Think on whether there is something in your makeup that makes you especially prone to this sin.

- **LONG**
Desire deliverance from the sin.

- **CONTEMPLATE**
Think on and figure out the occasions in which this sin breaks out and guard against them.

- **MEDITATE**
Pursue God in your thoughts to see his glory and your desperate inability. Think about God. Read his Word and meditate on it.

- **BATTLE**
Fight hard against the first awakenings of that sin. Never, ever allow yourself to play with sin.

- **EXPECT**
Desire to hear and know that God will speak peace to your soul (but do not speak it to yourself until he does).

STOPPING OLD HABITS

STARTING
NEW HABITS

PUTTING ON THE NEW

- **REPLACE**

  Where you have a certain vice in your life, an especially strong temptation to sin, or an especially strong history of sin, you will have to work extra hard to put that sin to death AND to put on the opposite virtue.

  - **PURSUE**

    We also need to generally pursue godly character. There are some areas where you are not particularly prone to sin, and in these areas, you need to generally pursue godliness.

CHAPTER SEVEN
PUTTING ON

One of the great joys and benefits of living in a multicultural city like Toronto is learning about cultures very different from my own. I recently attended a wedding that displayed both French-Canadian and Nigerian traditions, and it was fascinating to see the similarities and the differences between the two cultures. The two groups dressed completely differently and behaved completely differently. Where one family quietly filed into the room wearing solid and muted colors, the other burst in with dancing and brightly beautiful clothing. You can probably guess which was which.

Romans 8:29 tells us that "those whom [God] foreknew he also predestined to become conformed to the image of his Son." This is the great goal of the Christian life: to become like Christ. In our last chapter, we saw that the Bible talks about becoming like Christ through a couple of different word pictures. It talks about putting an old man to death and bringing a new man to life, and it talks about putting off old clothing and putting on new clothing. Just as Lazarus walked out of the tomb and began peeling off his grave clothes, we are to walk away from our spiritual deadness and put on spiritual life. In short, we need to stop living like dead men! This was our focus in the last chapter.

In this chapter, we want to talk about the other side of becoming like Christ. We must not only stop behaving in sinful ways, but we are also called to learn to think and to behave in righteous and holy ways. We not only take off the dead man's clothing, but we put on the living man's clothing. As a Christian, you cannot merely stop sinning. That is a great thing to do, but not sinning is not enough. You need to pursue the right things. You need to turn away from sin and turn toward righteousness. The Christian life is not only about what you cannot and must not do, but also about what you now can and need to do.

TRUE CHANGE

The story of the prodigal son is one of the finest short stories ever told and certainly one of the sweetest of Jesus' many parables. You are familiar with the story, I am sure.

It involves a young man who approaches his father and demands his inheritance. By demanding his inheritance, he is essentially wishing his father dead, wishing he could have the benefits that ought to be his only after his father is in the grave. It is as if he is

TRUE LIFE CHANGE

SPIRITUAL AWAKENING

TRUE REPENTANCE

RECEIVING FORGIVENESS

NEW BEHAVIOR

saying, "I wish you were dead so I could have your money. Since you're not dead, at least give me my money." Remarkably, Dad grants this young man his wish and gives him the money.

Not surprisingly, the money does not last long. The young man goes out and blows it all on wild and reckless living. He lives the high life, spending the equivalent of millions and millions of dollars until every penny is gone and he is left alone and destitute. All he has left to keep him company is his regret. With his pockets empty and his belly aching, he soon finds himself feeding pigs, doing the absolute worst and most menial job that society can offer. But this is what he has to do to keep himself from starving to death. He even finds himself looking wistfully at the pigs and fighting jealousy as he sees them gobbling their food.

But then he comes to himself. He comes to himself and remembers the love and the character of his father.

> But when he came to himself, he said, "How many of my father's hired servants have more than enough bread, but I perish here with hunger! I will arise and go to my father, and I will say to him, 'Father, I have sinned against heaven and before you. I am no longer worthy to be called your son. Treat me as one of your hired servants.'" And he arose and came to his father. But while he was still a long way off, his father saw him and felt compassion, and ran and embraced him and kissed him. And the son said to him, "Father, I have sinned against heaven and before you. I am no longer worthy to be called your son." But the father said to his servants, "Bring quickly the best robe, and put it on him, and put a ring on his hand, and shoes on his feet. And bring the fattened calf and kill it, and let us eat and celebrate. For this my son was dead, and is alive again; he was lost, and is found." And they began to celebrate. (Luke 15:17–24)

The prodigal gives us a great picture of true repentance, of true life change. I want to point out four marks of repentance because they highlight the very traits I know you want to see in your life.

SPIRITUAL AWAKENING

This man has been utterly lost in his sin. He has been so committed to his sin that it has blinded him to his foolishness. He has been behaving like a pagan and a fool. But then he suddenly comes to his senses. Actually, God brings him to his senses, and at that point, he is able to see his sin clearly. He is given the gift of insight — of seeing his condition, of seeing his fallenness. And you, too, if you are a Christian, have come to your senses. True life change begins with a spiritual awakening.

TRUE REPENTANCE

The prodigal son's spiritual awakening is followed by repentance, by seeking forgiveness and reconciliation. The son determines he will return to his father and beg for help. He takes the long road home, goes to his father, and admits his sin: "Father, I have sinned against heaven and before you" (verse 18). He shows that he regrets not only the consequences of his sin but the sin itself. This is the great distinction between true and false repentance. He is not distressed that his money is gone, and he is not distressed that he had to eat pig's food — not first or foremost. He is distressed that he has alienated himself from his father. What hurts worst at the end of it all is the distance he created from his father by sinning against him. True life change demands repentance.

NEW BEHAVIOR

The son admits his sin, but he does more. He says, "I am no longer worthy to be called your son." He even plans to say, "I don't need privilege. I don't need position. Just give me you. Be my father, and I don't care about anything else." He would rather be a servant in the house of his father than a rich man in a distant land. Do you see how far his heart has changed? He has not only repented of his pride but has begun to display humility as well. He not only has repented of his laziness but is now willing to work hard. He is a changed man. He is replacing sin with righteousness. True life change demands new behavior.

RECEIVING FORGIVENESS

Finally, we see him receiving his father's forgiveness. He receives his father's hug. He receives the ring and the robe and the shoes, those symbols of position and acceptance. There is no faux humility here, no attempt to throw those things off and play the martyr. He does not try to say, "No, I'm beyond forgiveness. I am wretched and wicked. Please punish me. Please hurt me." No, he receives the forgiveness of his father and knows that he has been fully restored. He believes his father and begins to live as if what his father tells him is true. True life change demands accepting God's forgiveness.

In the prodigal son, we have a great picture of what it means to turn away from sin and to turn toward holiness and righteousness. True change is not only admitting wrong and stopping doing what is wrong. It is far more than that, far more complete.

Let's talk about what it means to put on the new man or to put on those new clothes.

PUTTING ON THE NEW

In the last chapter, we looked at these words from Colossians 3:5: "Put to death therefore what is earthly in you: sexual immorality, impurity, passion, evil desire, and covetousness, which is idolatry." The passage does not end there. Paul does not conclude with a list of things we must not do. Instead, we find a second list of traits and behaviors — the kinds of traits and behaviors that Christians are meant to exemplify: "Put on then, as God's chosen ones, holy and beloved, compassionate hearts, kindness, humility, meekness, and patience, bearing with one another and, if one has a complaint against another, forgiving each other; as the Lord has forgiven you, so you also must forgive. And above all these put on love, which binds everything together in perfect harmony" (verses 12 – 14).

Becoming like Christ involves putting sin to death, *and* it involves bringing righteousness to life. As you become like Christ, you will need to put *off* some things, and you will need to put *on* other things. This is the consistent teaching of the New Testament: When you stop one behavior, you must begin another.

You know you need to put sin to death. You need to take off those old grave clothes. That is a good start, but it is not enough. You also need to begin living a righteous life. You do not address sin only by eradicating that sin but also by exemplifying the opposite behavior. The reality is that sin pushes out virtue. Sin replaces virtue with vice. You cannot be a generous thief, because theft displaces generosity. You cannot be a husband-loving adulterer, because adultery displaces your love for your husband. You cannot be an industrious lazybones, because laziness displaces industry.

In what remains of this chapter, I want to focus on two things we are called to when we determine we will put on righteousness. We need to act in one way toward those areas where we are especially tempted to sin; and we need to act in another way toward those areas where we are not especially tempted to sin. In other words, we need to *specifically* pursue some kinds of holiness and *generally* pursue other kinds.

SPECIFICALLY REPLACE VICE WITH VIRTUE

We all sin in different ways, and each of us is prone to different sins and temptations. Christians have often spoken about "besetting sins," those sins that are especially stubborn and deep-rooted—those sins that dominate our lives more than any other (Hebrews 12:1). You may find that your deepest struggles are with lying or stealing or lust. However, another Christian may struggle with very different sins and find it difficult to even imagine how you could ever struggle with the sins you agonize against every day. Each of us is different, and each of us struggles in different ways. What is common to us all, though, is deep-rooted battles against particular sins.

As you grow in Christlikeness, you need to identify those specific sins and put them to death. Where you have a certain vice in your life, a particularly powerful temptation to

SPIRITUAL DISCIPLINES

As Christians continue to "grow in the grace and knowledge of our Lord and Savior Jesus Christ" (2 Peter 3:18), they do so by listening to his Word (John 15:7), speaking to him in prayer (John 16:24), and loving others with their time and lives (John 13:35). Some practical ways believers can deepen their passion for God and express their love for others is by participating in corporate worship (Psalm 100:1 – 5), taking extended times of fasting and prayer (Matthew 6:16 – 18), and meeting the needs of others (2 Corinthians 8 – 9).

For further study, see:
Spiritual Disciplines for the Christian Life by Donald Whitney

sin, or an especially strong history of sin, you will have to work especially hard to put that sin to death and to put on the opposite virtue.

We often see this principle in Paul's epistles. In Ephesians 4, he commands the Christians in Ephesus to put off the old man with all its sin and unrighteousness and to put on the new man with all its holiness and righteousness (verses 22 – 24). And then he gives specific examples: "Let the thief no longer steal, but rather let him labor, doing honest work with his own hands, so that he may have something to share with anyone in need" (verse 28). Do you see it there? The thief needs to stop stealing, but that is not enough. The thief needs to stop stealing and instead learn to work hard, to earn a living, and to give generously. The thief will know he has put his sin to death and come alive to righteousness when, instead of stealing money, he is joyfully and generously giving away a portion of his money. That is a complete transformation.

Paul writes, "Let no corrupting talk come out of your mouths, but only such as is good for building up, as fits the occasion, that it may give grace to those who hear" (verse 29). There he shows us the very same principle. If your deep-rooted sin involves struggling with words and you continually find filthy words coming out of your mouth, you need to be convicted of your sinfulness, and you need to put that sin to death. But that is not all. You also need to learn to speak words that build up other people. The gossip will know she has put her sin to death and come alive to righteousness when, instead of speaking words that cut and destroy, she is speaking words that bring healing, comfort, and encouragement.

FRUIT OF THE SPIRIT

JOHN 14:27

PE
PEACE

εἰρήνη eiréné, i-ray´-nay; probably from a primary verb εἴρω eiró (to join); peace (literally or figuratively); by implication, prosperity: — one, peace, quietness, rest.

1 PETER 3:16

GE
GENTLENESS

πραΰτης prautés, prah-oo´-tace; mildness, i.e. (by implication), humility: — meekness.

1 CORINTHIANS 13:4-5

LV
LOVE

ἀγάπη agapé, ag-ah´-pay; love, i.e. affection or benevolence; specifically (plural) a love-feast: — (feast of) charity(-ably), dear, love.

ROMANS 15:13

JO
JOY

χαρά chara, khar-ah´; cheerfulness, i.e.,calm delight: — gladness, greatly (be exceeding), joy(-ful, -fully, -fulness, -ous).

3 JOHN 1:3

FA
FAITHFULNESS

πίστις pistis, pis´-tis; persuasion, i.e.,credence; moral conviction (of religious truth, or the truthfulness of God or a religious teacher), especially reliance upon Christ for salvation; abstractly, constancy in such profession; by extension, the system of religious (Gospel) truth itself: — assurance, belief, believe, faith, fidelity.

PSALM 75:2

PT
PATIENCE

μακροθυμία makrothumia, mak-roth-oo-mee´-ah; longanimity, i.e. (objectively),forbearance or (subjectively) fortitude: — longsuffering, patience.

ROMANS 15:14

GD
GOODNESS

ἀγαθωσύνη agathósuné, ag-ath-o-soo´-nay; goodness, i.e., virtue or beneficence: — goodness.

1 CORINTHIANS 9:24-27

SC
SELF-CONTROL

ἐγκράτεια egkrateia, eng-krat´-i-ah; self-control (especially continence): — temperance.

EPHESIANS 4:31-32

KI
KINDNESS

χρηστός chréstos, khrase-tos´; employed, i.e. (by implication), useful (in manner or morals): — better, easy, good(-ness), gracious, kind.

DEFINITIONS FROM STRONG'S EXHAUSTIVE CONCORDANCE

Where are you especially tempted to sin? When it comes to those vices that mark your life, you need to put those sins to death and then battle hard to put on the opposite virtues.

The man who has struggled with lust needs to stop lusting or needs to stop committing adultery. That's a great place to start, but it's not enough. He also needs to learn to put on self-control, learning to faithfully steward his sexuality to the glory of God. He will prove the power of God in him when he now rejoices to do what honors and glorifies God.

The person who battles with laziness cannot merely stop being lazy but must learn to be active and to use her gifts and abilities to be industrious and serve other people. And on and on it goes.

If your life is like a glass, that glass is always full. When you take something out, something else rushes in. When you stop sinning, it's like you've left a void in your life, and if you don't now fill it with something good, another sin will rush in to take its place. When focusing on putting sin to death, never neglect the discipline of bringing some new and opposite virtue to life.

Here's what Jesus says in Luke 11: "When the unclean spirit has gone out of a person, it passes through waterless places seeking rest, and finding none it says, 'I will return to my house from which I came.' And when it comes, it finds the house swept and put in order. Then it goes and brings seven other spirits more evil than itself, and they enter and dwell there. And the last state of that person is worse than the first" (verses 24 – 26).

That's why you can never leave yourself empty. Wherever you have a vice, a particularly stubborn and difficult sin, work hard to identify the opposite virtue and learn to put it on.

This is the first part of putting on the new man or the new clothes. But there is more.

GENERALLY PURSUE GODLY CHARACTER

You also need to generally pursue godly character. There are some areas where you are not particularly prone to sin, but even there, you still need to pursue godliness. Let me give a couple of examples from my own life.

There are certain sins that have been part of my life for as long as I can remember. When I was young, I had a problem with lying. I spoke lies so freely and frequently that I sometimes began to muddle fantasy with reality. Not only that, but I was convinced I was a good liar and that I could get away with anything. After I became a Christian, I had to learn to become a truth teller. I had to learn to love the truth and the value of always telling the truth. This is exactly what we have just considered — specifically replacing deep-rooted habits of sin with specific virtues.

There are other sins that have never really been a struggle for me. I have never struggled with stealing. I do not have to put a lot of effort into battling the sin of theft. It just isn't a significant temptation. However, this does not mean I never have to consider the sin of theft or the opposite virtue. I still need to pursue the virtue of generosity, and I still need to seek to grow in it. It may not receive as much effort or as much prayer. I may not enlist a mentor or accountability partner to help me there, but it still needs to receive attention. There is not a single virtue in the Bible that I am free to ignore as though it does not pertain to me.

God's call on you is to pursue godly character in all its forms and all its manifestations. This means you need to look for those traits and virtues that the Bible lauds.

Consider the fruit of the Spirit: "love, joy, peace, patience, kindness, goodness, faithfulness, gentleness, self-control" (Galatians 5:22 – 23). Do you exemplify each of these characteristics? How is your love? Do you love the people in your life more than you did a year ago? How would they know? I am not asking whether you *feel* more love for them, but whether you are *acting* in love toward them. This is what true love is — not mere thoughts but sacrificial actions. How is your self-control? Are you displaying self-control in your thoughts? Are you displaying self-control in your habits and your appetites? Have you asked others whether your life is marked by self-control?

And then consider the Beatitudes (Matthew 5). "Blessed are the meek, for they shall inherit the earth" (verse 5). Are you meek? Do you display meekness? Is meekness a growing or declining trait in your life? "Blessed are the peacemakers, for they shall be called sons of God" (verse 9). How are you doing in this virtue of peacemaking? Are you a fighter or a peacemaker? When people think of you, do they fear a fight, or do they know you'll be gentle and kind? What does your social media presence say about you?

Consider the book of James and its appeals to be careful with words: "From the same mouth come blessing and cursing. My brothers and sisters, these things ought not to be so" (James 3:10). What do your words reveal about your heart? Are you using your words responsibly? Are you showing growth and maturity here, or decline and immaturity?

Wherever you go in the Bible, you will find God telling you who you ought to be and how you ought to behave. And you are responsible before God for each one of these virtues.

But here is the beautiful thing: If you are living the Christian life, you will be constantly exposed to God's Word, and it will search your heart and mind and life. You will be sitting under the preaching of God's Word week after week as you attend worship services. You will be reading your Bible every day. You will be doing family devotions. You will be reading the Bible with friends. As you do these things, you will be constantly hearing what God requires from you. His Spirit will be constantly active through the Word. You will see all of those great traits and virtues and habits you need to put on, and the Spirit will give you a great longing to exemplify them.

CONCLUSION

God calls you to grow in your spiritual health, and one of the ways you obey his call is by putting on the new man, putting on the clothes that mark you as a Christian. You are called to *specific* obedience in the areas where you are particularly prone to sin. Look for those areas, and battle hard to learn to put on those new habits, new patterns, new desires, new joys. You will find far more joy and far longer-lasting joy in obedience than you ever did in your disobedience. And you are called to *general* obedience in all the other areas — even areas where you naturally excel.

Look specifically, look generally, and be like Christ. This is how you put on all those traits and characteristics that mark you as a Christian.

CHAPTER EIGHT
VOCATION

Let's take a moment to consider where we have traveled so far. In section one, you learned that Christians have the privilege of enjoying a relationship, a genuine friendship, with God. And like any friendship, this one requires each person to pursue the other. In the second section, you saw that you need to grow in your understanding of the work of Christ, both the great drama of what God is doing in this world and the doctrine of the Christian faith. In section three, you heard the call to become like Christ by putting off old patterns of sin and putting on new, righteous behaviors.

And now we come to this final section and have just one big topic left to consider: the lifelong challenge to live for Christ. God has granted you salvation through Jesus Christ, and in doing so, he has set you free to live a very different kind of life. Instead of living for yourself, for your own goals, for your own purposes, you are now free to live for a much higher and better ideal. You are free to live for Christ, for his goals and his purposes. This is the truest and best kind of freedom. And in the chapters ahead, we will look at a few of the ways you can do this.

LIVE AS YOU ARE CALLED

It is always one of the first questions we ask when we meet someone we have never met before: *What do you do?* We carry around in our heads a mental database of the people we know. For each of those people, we have a little profile that usually includes an image of their face, along with the most basic information — their name, the context in which we met them, and what they do. Part of the reason we like to know what people do is that their occupation is an important extension of their personality. Occupation reflects their values, their beliefs, their passions.

We know that the person who answers "I am an artist" is going to be very different from the person who answers "I am an engineer" or "I am a pastor." The woman who answers "I am a professional mixed martial artist" is going to be quite different from the woman who answers "I am a stay-at-home mom" or the one who answers "I am taking a few years to travel the world."

What we do is closely related to who we are. And as a Christian, you are responsible to give all of who you are and what you do to the Lord.

VOCATION

There are times when the Bible is sublimely practical. In his first letter to the church at Corinth, Paul offers this instruction: "Only let each person lead the life that the Lord has assigned to him, and to which God has called him" (1 Corinthians 7:17). This instruction implies that God has made each of us uniquely and assigned to us unique lives with unique roles. Our responsibility before God is to understand the gifts, the skills, and the passions he has given us and to use those in fitting ways — in ways that do good to others and, in turn, bring glory to God.

This is exactly why God has put us into this world: to bring glory to him by doing good to others. He says as much in Matthew 5:16: "Let your light shine before others, so that they may see your good works and give glory to your Father who is in heaven." Jesus' good friend Peter wrote, "Keep your conduct among the Gentiles honorable, so that when they speak against you as evildoers, they may see your good deeds and glorify God on the day of visitation" (1 Peter 2:12). There is a clear flow here: God gives us gifts; we use our gifts to do good to others; and through it all, God gets glory.

When you evaluate your gifts, skills, and passions, you are close to discovering what you might call your vocation or calling, the particular ways in which God means for you to glorify him by doing good to others.

Perhaps no contemporary Christian has done more to rediscover and celebrate the waning concept of vocation than Gene Edward Veith. Through his books and a host of articles, he has told Christians what their forebears already knew: The doctrine of vocation tells Christians how to live in this world. But it goes farther than that, to explain how God is at work in this world. He is at work through the people he has created.

> When we pray the Lord's Prayer, we ask God to give us this day our daily bread. And he does. The way he gives us our daily bread is through the vocations of farmers, millers, and bakers. We might add truck drivers, factory workers, bankers, warehouse attendants, and the lady at the checkout counter. Virtually every step of our whole economic system contributes to that piece of toast you had for breakfast. And when you thanked God for the food that he provided, you were right to do so.[26]

When you thank God for a piece of toast, you are not only thanking him for the food you are about to eat, but for the people, the skills, and the processes that got it from the field to the plate. You are acknowledging that God has provided through these remarkable means.

God chooses to bring about extraordinary provision through ordinary people and ordinary means. And this is exactly what God does in the world. God could have created all of humanity by drawing them out of the dust as he did Adam and Eve. Instead, he chose to work through the vocation of family, the ordinary means of mothers and fathers and sexual union. God protects us through his provision of government. God heals us through doctors and nurses. God teaches us his Word through preachers and teaches us facts through schoolteachers. "It is essential in grasping the magnitude of this teaching" writes Veith, "to understand first the sense in which vocation is God's work."[27] It is God's work completed through human beings.

We can advance one more step to see that God "is hidden in vocation." Our eyes show us the farmer as the provider of food, the doctor as the provider of health care, the pastor as the provider of spiritual nurture, and the driver as the provider of transport. But if we look at them through the lens of vocation, we will see that "God is genuinely present and active in what they do for us."[28] And you will see that God is genuinely present and active in what you do for them. You need to look at and live your own life through the lens of vocation.

I want to point to three important applications that provide essential guidance as you live for Christ in this world.

YOU HAVE MANY VOCATIONS

You do not have just one vocation, but many. A great misunderstanding about vocation is that each of us has just one: I am a pastor or I am a mechanic or I am a homemaker. But a thorough understanding of vocation teaches us that we all have many areas for which we are responsible before the Lord.

I am a citizen of Canada and have the vocation of citizen. I live in the town of Oakville, where I have the vocation of neighbor. I am married to Aileen and have the vocation of husband. Together we have three children, which assigns to me the vocation of father.

And then I hold the vocation of pastor at Grace Fellowship Church and the vocation of writer. My vocation is each of these and the sum of these. Individually and all together, they are a platform from God that allows me to extend to others the goodness and kindness of God on behalf of God. And whenever I do this, however I do this, God receives the glory.

You, too, have many vocations. You are a citizen, a son or daughter, a neighbor, a church member. You may also be a mother or father, a husband or wife, a worker or manager. Some of these vocations are more important than others. Some demand great swaths of your time, while some demand much less. But right there in the mix of them is your calling before God — who you should be and how you should live out the days God has given you.

No matter what your vocations are, they all carry the same great purpose: to do good to others and bring glory to God. Your purpose as a citizen of your country is to do good for others as a citizen and in that way to bring glory to God. Your purpose as a husband or wife is to serve your spouse, which brings glory to God. Your purpose as a friend is to do good to others and bring glory to God. As a Christian, you live outside yourself, joyfully doing all you can to bring good to others.

VOCATION BRINGS DIGNITY

The doctrine of vocation brings the utmost significance and dignity to your work. When we understand that vocation is extending the goodness and grace of God to others, to serve as the "mask of God,"[29] we understand that in a sense all vocations are equal. All of them have the highest dignity.

The dignity of work does not come from the amount of skill necessary to do the job. It does not come from the importance of that work for the functioning of a nation or society. The dignity of work comes from the source of that work, which is always God himself. The doctor who operates within the deepest recesses of the human brain is in the same line of work as the person who hauls away the trash from the end of the doctor's driveway. They are both working on behalf of God. They are both in the business of extending God's care to other people. Both have the choice to joyfully submit to God's will in vocation or to flee from it.

THE WORK OF A CHRIST FOLLOWER

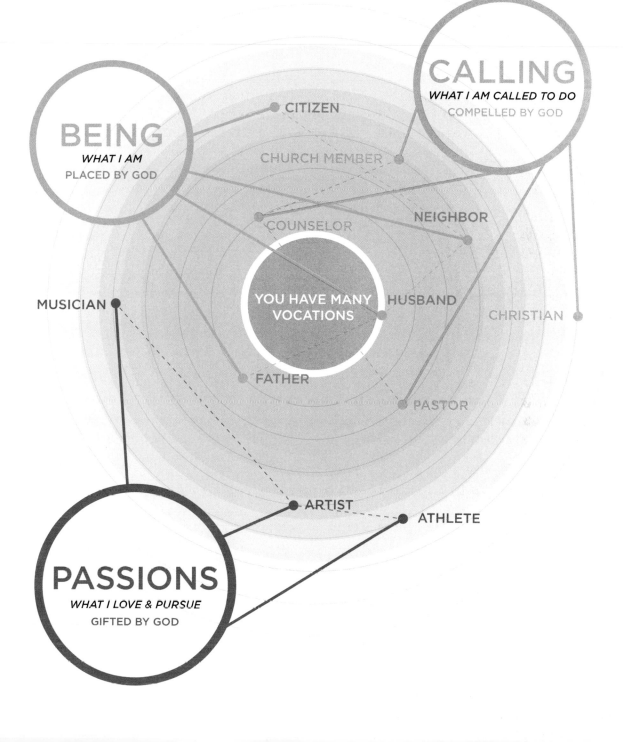

CALLING
WHAT I AM CALLED TO DO
COMPELLED BY GOD

BEING
WHAT I AM
PLACED BY GOD

CITIZEN

CHURCH MEMBER

NEIGHBOR

COUNSELOR

MUSICIAN

YOU HAVE MANY VOCATIONS

HUSBAND

CHRISTIAN

FATHER

PASTOR

ARTIST

ATHLETE

PASSIONS
WHAT I LOVE & PURSUE
GIFTED BY GOD

Let's focus briefly on the one vocation you might consider to be your job or your foremost responsibility in life. This is the one that might be part of your Facebook profile or be printed on a business card. My vocation is pastor. My wife's vocation is mother and homemaker. My co-elder Steve's vocation is airline pilot, and my friend Linda's vocation is executive director of a Pregnancy Care Center. Each of us has other responsibilities and other vocations, but these are the ones that consume the majority of our time and are often the ones that compensate us with a wage.

My wife and I have often spoken about her frustrations with her vocation of caring for our home and family. It is not that she has ever wanted to do anything else or that she feels trapped in a life she did not choose. It is simply that her work is difficult and repetitive and, in many ways, unrewarding. She lives in a cycle of tasks that she does not particularly enjoy — washing dishes, folding laundry, applying bandages to bloody knees, and providing emotional stability to a needy husband.

What brings help and hope is this doctrine of vocation — the fact that she is serving as a kind of conduit for the goodness and grace of God. When she fulfills her vocation, she is doing God's work on God's behalf. God wants us to bring order to a chaotic world, and Aileen brings godly orderliness when she keeps the home. God wants to care for those who are hurting, and Aileen brings his care and tenderness when she bandages a child's knee. God wants to extend help to men who are overwhelmed by life's circumstances, and he extends this help through her. She is the means of God's providential care.

And so are you in your vocation. If God has gifted you with a logical, orderly, mathematical mind, then you extend an aspect of God's concern for this world when you design buildings or bridges or software. If God has gifted you with an eye for color and an instinct for design, then you extend an aspect of God's concern for this world when you create beautiful art or design a slick new product branding. God could have arranged the world in such a way that he would do all of these good things himself. Instead, he assigned them to human beings, so you do this work on his behalf. Your vocation is your day-by-day opportunity to glorify God by serving others and, in that way, serve as a faithful representative of the God who glorifies himself by serving others.

MY VOCATION EXTENDS THE ORDER, GOODNESS, AND GRACE OF GOD TO OTHERS

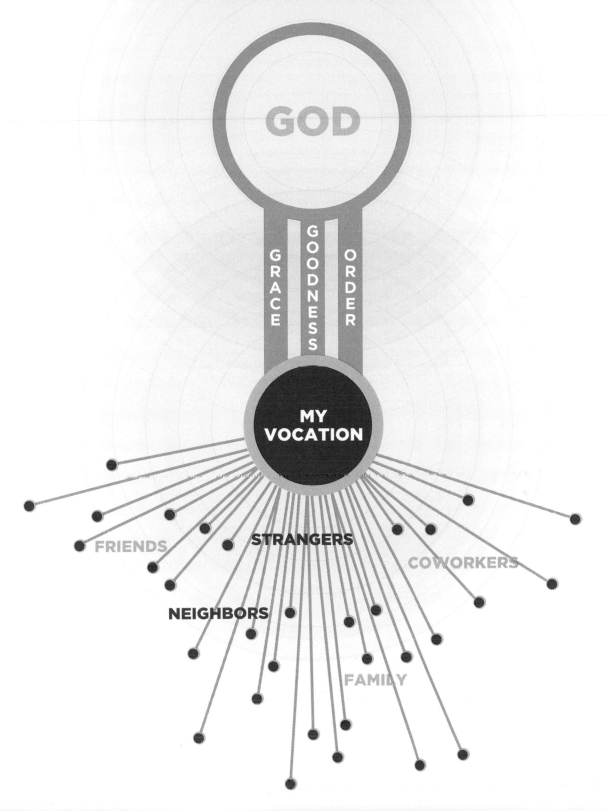

VOCATION LEADS TO WORSHIP

There is one more thing we should say about vocation, and it is this: Vocation leads to worship. It is meant to lead to worship. We worship God through vocation when we do the things God made us to do and when we observe other people doing what God made them to do.

Have you ever watched a mother carefully nurturing her child and caught just a glimpse, a reflection, of the love and care of God? Haven't you seen at least a glimpse of the mind of God in a beautiful design or a glimpse of the artistry of God in a great work of music or art? These glimpses are meant to draw you beyond themselves to worship and praise God himself. And these glimpses are meant to motivate you to joyfully carry out your vocation, to do God's work on God's behalf. You bring worship and glory to God when you serve others with the skills, gifts, and passions that God has given you. And you give opportunities for others to glorify God as they observe you working on his behalf.

Vocation also leads to worship when you praise God for the way he cares for you through others. You have no reason to look down on the man who picks up your trash each week. On the contrary, you have every reason to praise God for his care for you that is extended through that individual. When I am going through a particularly difficult time and my wife brings me comfort, it is really God bringing me comfort through this beautiful means he has provided. I ought to thank my wife, but ultimately, I ought to praise my God. The love and care and comfort I receive from her flows from the source of all-perfect love, care, and comfort. After all, "Every good gift and every perfect gift is from above, coming down from the Father

THE SOVEREIGNTY OF GOD

God rules over every aspect of his creation, from the most spectacular events (Isaiah 46:9–11; Daniel 4:34–35) to the smallest details (Proverbs 16:33; Matthew 10:29–30). Indeed, he works all things according to the counsel of his will (Romans 8:28; Ephesians 1:11). In his goodness, he is sovereign even over evil (Job 2:10; 42:11), although he himself does not tempt anyone to sin (James 1:13–17; 1 John 1:5). When man intends evil, God intends good (Genesis 50:20) and promises his people that all the suffering they endure for his sake is more than worth it (Romans 8:18; 2 Corinthians 4:17–18).

For further study, see:
The Sovereignty of God by A. W. Pink

of lights with whom there is no variation or shadow due to change" (James 1:17). She is the means, but he is the source.

Gene Edward Veith summarizes this truth well: "Thus, God is graciously at work, caring for the human race through the work of other human beings. Behind the care we have received from our parents, the education we received from our teachers, the benefits we receive from our spouse, our employers, and our government stands God himself, bestowing his blessings."[30] There are few miracles in this world because we need few miracles in this world. God moves through the most ordinary means in the most extraordinary ways.

CONCLUSION

Who has God made you to be? What gifts, skills, and passions has God given you? What roles and responsibilities has he assigned to you? Your vocations are found right there. Each one of them is to be done out of love for God and for the good of people he has created in his image.

CHAPTER NINE
RELATIONSHIPS

The Bible is a book about relationships. This is not unexpected, since in the Bible a relational God gives his self-revelation to relational beings. Ultimately, God's purpose in the Bible is to address the fractured and broken relationship between himself and man. In its pages, we learn that we were created to live in relationship with God, but that we deliberately rebelled against him, destroying the peace and harmony that had existed between us. We learn that God took action, meeting us in our helplessness by sending his Son, Jesus Christ. What God accomplished through the death and resurrection of Christ was a great act of reconciliation. In 2 Corinthians, Paul speaks of the gospel and writes, "All this is from God, who through Christ reconciled us to himself and gave us the ministry of reconciliation; that is, in Christ God was reconciling the world to himself, not counting their trespasses against them, and entrusting to us the message of reconciliation" (5:18 – 19). Each use of the word *reconciliation* points us to the restoration of broken relationships.

Through the gospel, God has reconciled us to himself, restoring the relationship between us. And now, as we live out the gospel, we serve as ambassadors of reconciliation — building, maintaining, and repairing relationships with others. For this reason, the Bible continually addresses those relationships. Jesus addressed relationships in his teaching and parables, and the apostles addressed them in their teaching and epistles.

We live in constant relationship with others. We are born into an existing relationship with parents and siblings and soon develop many more. Some of these are peer relationships, but the ones that the Bible takes special care to address are those in which each person plays a different role and especially in which God means for there to be a pattern of leadership and submission.

God made this world hierarchical. He is the preexisting and all-powerful God who created all, who owns all, who rules all. Everyone and everything in this world is to bow the knee before him in humble obedience and submission. For the sake of order, and in order to reflect his authority, he created patterns of leading and following, roles that would involve exercising authority and roles that would involve submitting to authority. Each one of us takes on both of those roles at different times and in different contexts.

While leadership is a popular word today and is the subject of tens of thousands of books, the flip side of leadership — submission — is much less popular. Yet one cannot exist without the other. Leadership without submission is chaos and anarchy. While some of us are called to lead some of the time, all of us are called to submit all of the time. God defines both of these terms in his own way.

When God calls for leadership, he calls for a particular kind — what we refer to as servant leadership. Christians are to lead in such a way that they pursue the good of others ahead of their own good. When God calls for submission, he also calls for a special kind — willing and joyful submission that understands submitting to a human authority as an extension of submitting to God's authority.

There is one important caveat: Because all authority is ultimately delegated by God, no one has the right to require what God does not require or to demand what he forbids. We are to obey authority where it exists, except for those times when a lesser authority contradicts a higher authority. So, for example, we are to submit to government in general, but we must resist government when it demands that we disobey God. (See, for example, the exemplary actions of Shadrach, Meshach, and Abednego in Daniel 3.)

GOVERNMENTS AND CITIZENS

The New Testament was written at a time and in a context of oppression. When Jesus came into this world, the concern of most Jews was not for a Savior to deliver them from their sin, but for a warrior to deliver them from Roman oppression. When Paul was embarking on missionary journeys and writing his letters, he was sometimes doing so from behind the cold iron bars of a Roman prison. This government was dominant and brutal, maintaining its brand of peace by ruthlessly stamping out any hint of rebellion. Many of the early Christians were Jews who had long been oppressed and subjugated by this government.

It is little wonder, then, that the New Testament has to address the relationship of governments to citizens. God makes it clear that government is a gift of God that exists to do the will of God. Citizens are to submit to government as an expression of their submission to God. You are a citizen of your nation and called to submit to the lawful authorities over you.

In his letter to the Christians at Rome, Paul writes, "There is no authority except from God, and those that exist have been instituted by God" (Romans 13:1). Governments exist and rule with an authority that has been delegated to them by God. Paul goes on to show that governments exist to maintain peace and order and even to collect taxes. The justice of the government is an extension of the justice of God. The best government is the one that rules with an understanding of its responsibility before God and with a desire to reflect his rule.

Christian, you are called to joyfully submit to the rule of government: "Let every person be subject to the governing authorities ... [because] whoever resists the authorities resists what God has appointed, and those who resist will incur judgment" (Romans 13:1 – 2). You are to express your submission to God by giving to the government what it asks of you: "taxes to whom taxes are owed, revenue to whom revenue is owed, respect to whom respect is owed, honor to whom honor is owed" (Romans 13:7). Christians are to joyfully submit to government, knowing that they are, in fact, submitting to God. Vote in elections, obey the laws of the land, and pay your taxes with a smile. Do so in obedience to God.

BOSSES AND EMPLOYEES

The New Testament was written at a time of government oppression, but also at a time of personal oppression. Roman society permitted a form of slavery. It was not an exact equal to the kind of racial slavery that was a feature of early American history and not an exact equal to the sexual slavery that exists in too many places in the world today. But it was slavery nonetheless, the ownership of one person by another. The New Testament writers often addressed slaves and their masters. Today, we extend those instructions to speak to the relationships between employers and their employees. Here we see the same pattern of servant leadership and joyful submission.

HOW RELATIONSHIPS WORK

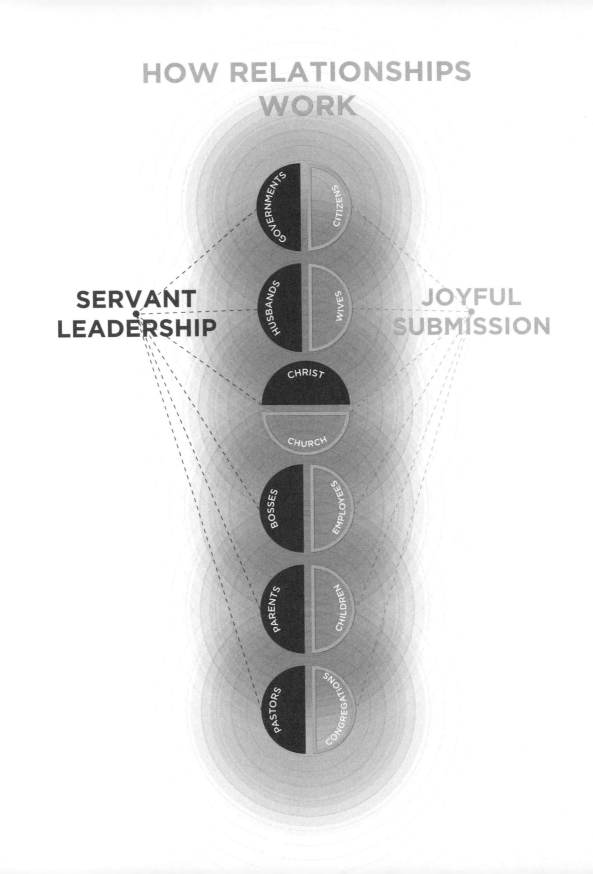

SERVANT LEADERSHIP

JOYFUL SUBMISSION

GOVERNMENTS

CITIZENS

HUSBANDS

WIVES

CHRIST

CHURCH

BOSSES

EMPLOYEES

PARENTS

CHILDREN

PASTORS

CONGREGATIONS

The consistent call to slaves was to submit to their masters, to do their absolute best work for the masters, and to see their service of their masters as an extension of their service to Christ. Paul's instruction in Ephesians 6 is typical: "Bondservants, obey your earthly masters with fear and trembling, with a sincere heart, as you would Christ, not by the way of eye-service, as people-pleasers, but as bondservants of Christ, doing the will of God from the heart, rendering service with a good will as to the Lord and not to man, knowing that whatever good anyone does, this he will receive back from the Lord, whether he is a bondservant or is free" (verses 5 – 8). Slaves and employees are to do their work with skill and effort, to submit to their bosses in the same way they submit to God.

Paul goes on to speak to masters, telling them to treat their slaves with the utmost dignity: "Masters, do the same to them, and stop your threatening, knowing that he who is both their Master and yours is in heaven, and that there is no partiality with him" (verse 9). Masters and bosses are to see the way in which God gently and lovingly leads us and then imitate him. They are not to lead by brutality and threats but by gentle example.

It bears mention that we should not take Paul's instructions as an endorsement of slavery as much as a simple acknowledgment of its existence. In fact, Paul would have been the first to acknowledge that the Bible contains within it the seeds of the destruction of slavery. In another letter, Paul writes, "For as many of you as were baptized into Christ have put on Christ. There is neither Jew nor Greek, there is neither slave nor free, there is no male and female, for you are all one in Christ Jesus" (Galatians 3:27 – 28). Where the Christian ethic reigned, slavery was doomed. But Paul's purpose in these letters was not to speak to slavery but to speak to slaves and their masters.

PASTORS AND CONGREGATIONS

Another foundational relationship of every Christian is that of the pastors to their congregations, the shepherds to the sheep in their care. The very same pattern of leadership and submission exists here.

Several New Testament epistles speak to the qualifications for a man who would be a pastor. It is remarkable that, of the more than twenty qualifiers, only one deals with skill ("able to teach"). All of the others deal with character. Men are qualified to hold the office of elder or pastor through Christian character more than skill. This character allows them to exemplify the kind of care that Christ provides for his people. They are to lead their people willingly rather than under compulsion (1 Peter 5:2) and to lead with gentleness and without domineering (1 Peter 5:3). They are to gently lead God's people by training them to do the work of ministry (Ephesians 4:11 – 13), guiding them into godly maturity.

Meanwhile, the members of a congregation are to love and to honor their pastors, to hold them in high esteem, and to care for their needs (1 Timothy 5:17 – 18). They are to show an extra measure of care in entertaining any kind of charge against a pastor (1 Timothy 5:19). The author of Hebrews puts it well: "Obey your leaders and submit to them, for they are keeping watch over your souls, as those who will have to give an account. Let them do this with joy and not with groaning, for that would be of no advantage to you" (Hebrews 13:17).

Pastors are to lead God's church in God's way while joyfully caring for God's people. Churches are to joyfully submit to their pastors, acknowledging those leaders as representing God's care and provision over them.

HUSBANDS AND WIVES

God's pattern of authority and submission carries even into the marriage relationship, and he has instructions to give us on how husbands and wives should relate to one another. In Ephesians 5:22, Paul speaks to wives: "Wives, submit to your own husbands, as to the Lord." In verse 25, he reciprocates with a command for husbands: "Husbands, love your wives, as Christ loved the church and gave himself up for her." Within the marriage relationship, God expects that a husband will lovingly lead his wife and that a wife will willingly submit to her husband's leadership.

He grounds this pattern in the creation of humanity, quoting from the book of Genesis: "Therefore a man shall leave his father and mother and hold fast to his wife, and the two shall become one flesh" (Ephesians 5:31; cf. Genesis 2:24). But he goes on to provide an unexpected surprise: Since the beginning of time, there has been a mystery hidden within marriage. "This mystery is profound, and I am saying that it refers to Christ and the church" (Ephesians 5:32).

Paul tells us that marriage exists to serve as a kind of portrait of Christ's relationship with the church. Just as Christ showed his love for and leadership of the church by giving up his life for her, husbands are to give up their very lives in service to their wives. And just as the church responds to Christ's love by gladly submitting to his leadership, wives are to respond to their husbands by joyfully submitting to their husbands. Here, too, we see the pattern of servant leadership and glad submission.

PARENTS AND CHILDREN

It will not surprise you that God's pattern of authority and submission extends to the relationship between parents and their children. These parent-child relationships are simply a reflection of the parent-child relationship we share with God.

In Ephesians 6, Paul directs a few words at children: "Children, obey your parents in the Lord, for this is right. 'Honor your father and mother' (this is the first commandment with a promise), 'that it may go well with you and that you may live long in the land'" (verses 1–3). He looks back to the Ten Commandments, given centuries earlier to the Israelites, and sees a pattern that extends across the ages: Children are to joyfully submit to their parents. Their submission to their parents is an extension of their submission to God.

Then Paul turns to parents, to fathers in particular, and writes, "Fathers, do not provoke your children to anger, but bring them up in the discipline and instruction of the Lord" (verse 4). Parents are to lead their children — and to do so particularly by teaching them who God is and what he requires of them. Parents are to lead their children gently and

LOVE

JOHN 13:34; JOHN 15:12; JOHN 15:17;
ROM 13:8; 1 THESS 4:9; HEB 13:1;
1 PET 1:22; 1 PET 3:8; 1 PET 4:8;
1 JOHN 3:11; 1 JOHN 3:14; 1 JOHN 3:23;
1 JOHN 4:7; 1 JOHN 4:11; 2 JOHN 5

ENCOURAGE

2 COR 13:11
1 THESS 4:18
1 THESS 5:11
HEB 3:13
HEB 10:25

BE HUMBLE

EPH 4:2
1 PET 3:8
1 PET 5:5

HAVE COMPASSION

EPH 4:32
1 PET 3:8

GREET

ROM 16:16
1 COR 16:20
2 COR 13:12
1 PET 5:14

LIVE IN PEACE

MARK 9:50
1 THESS 5:13

DON'T PAY BACK WRONG

1 THESS 5:15

CONFESS TO

JAMES 5:16

ACCEPT

ROM 15:7

BEAR IN LOVE

EPH 4:2
COL 3:13

SERVE

GAL 5:13

ADMONISH

COL 3:16

BE SYMPATHETIC

1 PET 3:8

BUILD UP

1 THESS 5:11

AGREE

1 COR 1:10

OFFER HOSPITALITY

1 PET 4:9

SUBMIT

EPH 5:21

LIVE IN HARMONY

ROM 12:16

DO GOOD

1 THESS 5:15

BE DEVOTED

ROM 12:10

SPUR TO LOVE

HEB 10:24

DON'T GRUMBLE

JAMES 5:9

FORGIVE

EPH 4:32
COL 3:13

DON'T LIE

COL 3:9

BE LIKE-MINDED

1 PET 3:8

DON'T PROVOKE

GAL 5:26

INSTRUCT

ROM 15:14

DON'T JUDGE

ROM 14:13

SPEAK SONGS TO

EPH 5:19

HAVE EQUAL CONCERN

1 COR 12:25

HONOR

ROM 12:10

HAVE THE MIND OF CHRIST

ROM 15:5
PHI 2:5

DON'T SLANDER

JAMES 4:11

PRAY FOR

JAMES 5:16

BE KIND

EPH 4:32

DON'T DEPRIVE

1 COR 7:5

BE PATIENT

EPH 4:2

SPUR TO GOOD DEEDS

HEB 10:24

BE GENTLE

EPH 4:2

THE NEW TESTAMENT COMMANDS US TO TREAT *ONE ANOTHER*
WITH LOVE, HUMILITY, AND RESPECT.
WE ARE ALSO TO ENCOURAGE *ONE ANOTHER* AND BE UNIFIED,

lovingly, not through brute force and intimidation. They are to see how God loves and leads them and to imitate him in their care for their children. Parents obey God by teaching their children to obey them.

FRIENDS

Every one of the relationships we have examined so far is a relationship that involves authority and submission. These are the relationships that merit special attention in the New Testament. But, of course, we also enjoy peer relationships in which we relate as friends. The Bible speaks to such relationships as well.

It often describes and displays close friendships — David and Jonathan, Jesus and John, and many others. It calls on us to build distinctly spiritual friendships that exist for the good of the other person. It is in the context of friendship, and perhaps especially friendships between members of the same local church, where we can carry out the many "one another" commands that pervade the New Testament: to build up one another (Romans 14:19), to confess our sins to one another (James 5:16), to encourage one another (1 Thessalonians 4:18), to both weep and rejoice with one another (Romans 12:15), and so many more. It is here, as friends, that we have the privilege of imitating the God who has become our friend (John 15:15).

SPIRITUAL LEADERSHIP

Jesus taught his disciples that the greatest among us is the servant of all (Matthew 23:11; Mark 9:35). That principle applies especially to leadership. While husbands are to lead their wives (Ephesians 5:22 – 33), fathers are to lead their children (Ephesians 6:1 – 4), and masters are to lead their servants (Ephesians 6:5 – 9), all Christians are to humbly submit to one another (Ephesians 5:21). The example that Christ leaves us is one of great power expressed through lowly, sacrificial service (John 13:1 – 17).

For further study, see:
Spiritual Leadership: A Commitment to Excellence for Every Believer by J. Oswald Sanders

CONCLUSION

Our relational God has reconciled us to himself. And now that he has reconciled us to himself, he gives us the great privilege and responsibility of extending relationships to others. We imitate Christ in his loving leadership. We imitate Christ in his servant-hearted submission. We imitate Christ in his deep, spiritual friendships. We live for him, through him, and in imitation of him.

SECTION FOUR
LIVE FOR CHRIST

CHAPTER TEN
STEWARDSHIP

You don't own it. Any of it. It all belongs to God. It belongs to God, even if you have a receipt for its purchase or your name is stamped on it. It is still his. The question is, will you treat it like you own it — or will you acknowledge that you are managing it on his behalf? This is the question of stewardship, and it is a question that makes all the difference.

You may know the word *steward* from air or rail travel. The steward is the person charged with caring for you while you are on board. But the word's original meaning goes a bit beyond that.

Imagine you are a wealthy estate owner and have decided to go away for a time. Before you depart, you appoint a steward to manage your affairs. His responsibility is to oversee your estate and to make decisions on your behalf. When the time came to make an important decision, this steward would be charged with attempting to determine what you would want to do in a given situation and then to act in a way consistent with your wishes. The more he knows about you, the better those decisions will be. The more he loves you, the purer those decisions will be. When you return from your journey, you have every right to demand an accounting from him, to evaluate his work. If he is a faithful steward, you should return to find everything safe and in good order. You may even find that everything is improved — that your estate has grown and that your wealth has increased. If he is an unfaithful steward, you may return to find devastation, disorder, and even poverty.

God has appointed you to be a steward of his world. Stewardship speaks to the relationship between you and the rest of what God has created — between you and God's gifts. Your stewardship extends to almost everything. If God made it, and if you have access to it, you are to be a steward of it. This principle is true of money and possessions, of talents and relationships. It is true of your body, your mind, your sexuality. It is true of the world around you. It *all* belongs to God, and he has entrusted it to you.

The principle of stewardship is built on two simple premises: God owns it, and you manage it.

God owns it. Because God created this world and everything in it, God owns this world and everything in it. It is tough to deny the logic! In Deuteronomy 10, we read, "To the LORD your God belong heaven and the heaven of heavens, the earth with all that is in

STEWARDSHIP

GOD OWNS IT
I MANAGE IT

it" (verse 14). The word *all* is no exaggeration. There is nothing in this world that falls outside the ownership of God. You bring nothing into this world; you take nothing out of this world; and strictly speaking, you own nothing in between. All that you possess is actually owned by God, who simply loans it to you for a time.

You manage it. God owns it all, but he delegates the management to you. God gives you what is his, and he instructs you to use those things well, to use them in ways that are consistent with his desires and his purposes. We see this mandate from the very beginning of time, when God created the world and then created human beings and immediately assigned them this job: "Be fruitful and multiply and fill the earth and subdue it, and have dominion over the fish of the sea and over the birds of the heavens and over every living thing that moves on the earth" (Genesis 1:28). Man was to represent God in filling this earth and exercising dominion over it.

We also know that God's desire is for people everywhere to hear the gospel and turn to Christ in repentance and faith (1 Timothy 2:4). Once again, he has assigned this responsibility to his people. It is not that God is incapable of doing this work on his own. No, it is simply his joy to delegate this responsibility to others.

The difference between an owner and a steward is essentially accountability. The steward is accountable to the owner, and the owner is accountable to himself. Let's look together at a few examples of areas where we are to serve as stewards.

MONEY AND POSSESSIONS

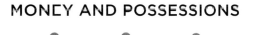

Few things in this world have a deeper hold on us than money and possessions. Few things provide a deeper sense of security and a deeper sense of fulfillment. The more of it we have, the safer and more important we feel. Because this is true, it comes as no surprise that the way you relate to your money tells an awful lot about your spiritual health and maturity.

We have learned already that God created this world and the human beings who inhabit it, and he told them to relate to it as its managers. Man was to tend not just the trees and animals, but the whole world. He was to create cities and cultures and, of course, economics and production and distribution and money. Money is one of the ways you fulfill your creation mandate to subdue the earth. What this means, of course, is that God is the owner of your money, and you are a steward over it. You live under God but above money, and your task as a steward is to use it faithfully. What is true of your money is equally true of your possessions. They, too, are owned by God because in some way they also originate in his provision and kindness.

Knowing that you are the manager of God's money makes every bit of difference to the way you relate to your money and to the possessions you buy with it.

STEWARDSHIP CALLS YOU TO FOCUS ON THE GOSPEL

One reason money can have such a grip on you is that it provides a convenient (though misguided) measure of your value. You may tend to believe your significance is directly related to your wealth. When you do not have money and do not have nice possessions, you may be prone to feel unloved and unimportant. But the gospel does not allow you to measure your worth or the depth of God's love by your money. The gospel assures you that each of us is equally favored by God and that your value is displayed in Christ's willingly giving up his life for you. Your value is found in your relationship with him, not in the number of your possessions or in the size of your bank account.

STEWARDSHIP CALLS YOU TO SEEK WISDOM

Those of us who live in the developed world enjoy unprecedented wealth and comfort. But it is never enough. We are addicted to debt, believing we can (and perhaps should) borrow money any time we decide we need something else. We are equally addicted to instant gratification — to seeing a shiny new gadget online, clicking Buy, and having it in our hands the very next day. Behind it all is a kind of materialism that teaches us that the only things that really matter are the things we can own and possess here on earth. Those three forces combine to cause us to tragically misuse our money. But an understanding of stewardship motivates us to seek wisdom and to use every penny as if God himself will require an accounting for it.

STEWARDSHIP CALLS YOU TO GIVE GENEROUSLY

When we release our ownership over money, we are freed to be generous with it. One of the ways God asks us to prove our stewardship over money is by giving some of it away. In the Old Testament, God's people were expected to tithe — to give the first and best 10 percent of their wealth to God for his purposes. And in the New Testament, this principle, though perhaps not the actual amount, carries on. When I give away a significant portion of my money, I am declaring my trust in God and in his ability to provide. I am effectively saying to God, "I will give away a part of it and trust that you will keep on providing." On the other hand, holding tightly to all of my money is a tacit declaration to God that I cannot trust him to provide. In this way, giving away a generous portion of what God has given me is an act of worship and a declaration of my faith in the character and provision of God. It is a matter of simple obedience, of returning to God what is already his.

STEWARDSHIP CALLS YOU TO INVEST IN ETERNITY

Jesus said, "Do not lay up for yourselves treasures on earth, where moth and rust destroy and where thieves break in and steal, but lay up for yourselves treasures in heaven, where neither moth nor rust destroys and where thieves do not break in and steal" (Matthew 6:19 – 20). Randy Alcorn echoes this truth with what he calls the treasure principle: You can't take it with you — but you *can* send it on ahead.[31] God has determined there will be an eternal relationship between you and your stuff, between you and your money. You can use your money in such a way that you forgo whatever pleasures you might enjoy on this earth in place of eternal treasures that God will give you as a reward for your faithfulness.

God does not call you to a life of endless frugality. He does not look down on you for buying the stuff you need or even for buying nice stuff. But he does call you to be wise, to be generous, and to be mindful that there is eternal value in using your money for his purposes.

BODY

I do not know of a concept that is more radically opposed to our cultural ethos than this one: Your body does not belong to you. Your body is not really yours at all. The right to an elective abortion has been premised on the understanding that a woman has the authority to decide what she wants to do with her own body. The rising acceptance of euthanasia is equally dependent on man owning his own body and being able to decide whether he will live or die. Yet God speaks this bold word into our cultural confusion: "You are not your own, for you were bought with a price. So glorify God in your body" (1 Corinthians 6:19 – 20). As a Christian, you need to understand that even your own body is not your own. Your body was created by God; it is owned by God; and it is to be used for God's purposes. You are merely a steward of the body you possess.

This reality calls you to relate to your body in certain ways.

JOYFUL FITNESS

I opened this book by describing my first foray into personal fitness. In large part, my decision to get fit was based on my growing understanding that God tells me to care for the body he entrusted to me. It is not my body, but his. And I know this body (and the soul and mind it contains) functions far, far better through fitness than sloth. The ancient gnostic movement, which has made a surprising twenty-first-century return, tells you that the soul and mind are good, while the body is evil. If this thinking is true, you can neglect the body and focus all of your attention on the mind. But the Bible teaches no such distinction. While your body will inevitably grow old and eventually die, you must still care for it and tend to its needs. Do you care for the body God has given you? Do you treat it like it belongs to him, not you?

JOYFUL MARTYRDOM

As a Christian, you need to care for your body, but you can also willingly give it up. Christian missionaries through the ages have faced disease and death for the sake of the gospel. Helen Roseveare was serving as a missionary in Africa when her house was raided, and she was raped and arrested. Noël Piper writes of Helen's response, "She writes movingly of how abandoned she felt that night. 'My God, my God, why have you forsaken me?' His answer to her was a removal of the fear as if it had been rinsed out of her — and a strong sense of his arms around her, holding her and comforting her. She felt as if he were saying, 'When I called you to myself, I called you to the fellowship of my suffering. They are not attacking you. They are attacking me. I'm just using your body to show myself to the people around you.' "[32]

During her captivity, shortly before her rescue, Helen was held in a room filled with other women. Soldiers began dragging women from the room and systematically raping them. Helen walked from the back of the line to the front of the line, willingly giving up her body in the hope that doing so might preserve another person from facing such an atrocity. I believe this sacrificial act pleased God, even though it caused harm to Helen's body.

Many more Christian missionaries have faced death rather than deny their faith. And this decision has been to exercise faithful stewardship of their bodies, willingly giving for the sake of the Lord what was his all along. They used their bodies to display his glory.

JOYFUL PURITY

Christians also serve as stewards of their sexuality and joyfully pursue purity. This pursuit is so important and so countercultural that I will devote an entire section to it.

SEXUALITY

Closely related to God's ownership of your body is God's ownership of your sexuality. God has given sexuality as a gift to humanity, and his plan is that it be expressed only and often between a husband and a wife within the bond of marriage. When used in this way, sexuality has the power to bind a husband and wife into a uniquely powerful union, while also generating more of his image bearers through procreation.

Yet ever since humans were plunged into sin, they have determined they will use sex for their own purposes rather than God's. They will misuse this gift. There are few areas where humans more gleefully declare their hatred of God and his ways than in misusing

STEWARDSHIP

YOU DON'T OWN ANYTHING.

GOD OWNS EVERYTHING.

IF GOD MADE IT AND YOU HAVE ACCESS TO IT, YOU ARE A STEWARD.

YOU ARE ACCOUNTABLE TO GOD FOR HOW YOU WORK WITH WHAT GOD OWNS [EVERYTHING].

HOW CAN I BE A GOOD STEWARD?

FOCUS ON THE GOSPEL

SEEK WISDOM

INVEST IN ETERNITY

	FOCUS ON THE GOSPEL	SEEK WISDOM	INVEST IN ETERNITY

MONEY

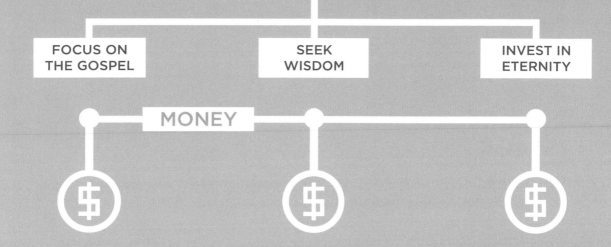

FOCUS ON THE GOSPEL: Our value is not tied to our money. The gospel tells us we are all valued equally and that value is demonstrated by Jesus in giving up his life for us.

SEEK WISDOM: Material wealth is a trap and can be very deceiving as we are addicted to more. We need to pray, read Proverbs, and learn from other financially savvy Christians.

INVEST IN ETERNITY: God demands a return on his investment. An owner doesn't give his money to a steward to lose it. We need to give generously to others and understand that we can't take it with us after we die.

BODY

FOCUS ON THE GOSPEL: We were bought with a price. Our bodies do not belong to us. The gospel tells us we don't need to provide them every pleasure to experience joy and peace.

SEEK WISDOM: We must seek wisdom on how to steward our bodies because our culture tells us we own them. We have been told we hold all the cards and even get to decide whether our body lives or dies.

INVEST IN ETERNITY: We are to train and protect our bodies because God values them as the temple of the Holy Spirit. We are commanded to sacrifice our bodies and to serve others. Therefore we must care for them well.

CHILDREN

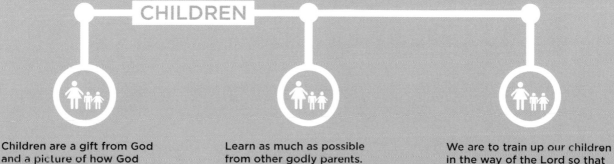

FOCUS ON THE GOSPEL: Children are a gift from God and a picture of how God sacrifices selflessly for us. We don't expect our children to provide the joy that only Jesus gives.

SEEK WISDOM: Learn as much as possible from other godly parents. Listen and watch them. Read good books and pray constantly for wisdom.

INVEST IN ETERNITY: We are to train up our children in the way of the Lord so that they might be saved and then train up future generations.

the gift of sexuality. The widespread acceptance of homosexuality depends on the understanding that I am the owner of my sexuality and that I am the one who decides how I will express myself. The rise of pornography is premised on the very same idea — that my sexuality is my own and that I am free to express it with a flesh-and-blood spouse or a screen-and-pixel image.

But again, the Bible speaks: "You are not your own, for you were bought with a price. So glorify God in your body" (1 Corinthians 6:19 – 20). Your body is not your own, and your sexuality is not your own. You are merely the steward of these gifts. God expects "that each one of you know how to control his own body in holiness and honor, not in the passion of lust like the Gentiles who do not know God" (1 Thessalonians 4:4 – 5).

To control your body in holiness and honor is to allow God to direct your sexuality. If you are unmarried, he calls you to refrain from all forms of sexuality. You are to treat "younger men as brothers, older women as mothers, younger women as sisters, in all purity" (1 Timothy 5:1 – 2). You are to willingly forgo sexual pleasure to find greater satisfaction in obedience. If you are married, you express stewardship over your body by forsaking all other means and mediums of sexual pleasure and instead willingly and regularly giving your body to your spouse for his or her pleasure and fulfillment (1 Corinthians 7:1 – 5). You surrender what is most private and most intimate for the good of the other and for the glory of God.

ENVIRONMENT

One of the foremost concerns of the wider culture today is the environment and our care for our planet. Many people are asking whether our current way of living is sustainable or whether we are destroying the planet for the sake of short-term pleasures. What will we leave to future generations?

As Christians, we know that God is the Creator of this planet and we are his deputies, his stewards, who have been charged with caring for it and exercising dominion over it. This reality means we ought to be at the forefront of creation care. We, of all people, should be concerned for the planet that God has created for us and assigned to us. We, of all people, should know we have the tendency to misuse God's gifts. We misuse money and possessions, our bodies and our sexuality. So why would it be any different with our planet?

As Christians, we can affirm that God means for us to spread across the planet to populate it, to discover it, and to exploit its riches (Genesis 1:26–28). We can affirm that a day will come when God will remake and renew this planet in such a way that he will remove all the traces of sin that pollute it (Revelation 21:1–4). But we can also affirm that we have no right to pillage it at the expense of future generations and that we should make it our aim to leave it in better condition than we found it. Francis Schaeffer once wrote, "By creation man has dominion, but as a fallen creature he has used that dominion wrongly. Because he is fallen, he exploits created things as though they were nothing in themselves, and as though he has an autonomous right to them."[33]

We are stewards of this planet and of this world. We are charged by God to care for it well and to use its riches to carry out God's purposes.

GOSPEL

Perhaps our most important stewardship of all is the stewardship of the gospel. And I cannot think of a more fitting place to end this book.

As Jesus left this earth, he gave his disciples and his church this instruction: "Go therefore and make disciples of all nations, baptizing them in the name of the Father and of the Son and of the Holy Spirit, teaching them to observe all that I have commanded you. And behold, I am with you always, to the end of the age" (Matthew 28:19–20). When you read the early history of the church in the book of Acts and when you read the New Testament epistles, you can't help but see how seriously Christians took this charge. They understood that God had made them stewards of the good news of Jesus Christ. And they gave all they had to ensure they were good and faithful stewards. It is because of their faithful stewardship that the gospel spread through the years and the generations until it spread to me and to you. You are a Christian only because other Christians were faithful stewards of the gospel.

You faithfully steward the gospel when you protect it and when you spread it.

You protect the gospel by growing in spiritual health and maturity. Paul told his young protégé Timothy to "guard the good deposit entrusted to you" (2 Timothy 1:14). Paul told Timothy that, as a Christian, he was responsible before God to understand, believe, and protect the gospel. That is true of you as well. The more you know of God and his gospel and the more you know of the Bible and of Christian doctrine, the greater your ability to identify any deviations or counterfeits. The call to grow in health is not only a call for you to do what is best for you, but a call for you to do what is best for others. The gospel is always under attack and the more you know of it, the greater your ability to protect it.

You also protect the gospel by spreading it. There might be a temptation to guard the gospel by locking it up and sealing it away, but the better way is to spread it so much that it becomes impossible to stop. Just think of how the Bible spread. If there had been one Bible and it had been kept under lock and key, it would inevitably have been lost to history. Instead, Christians diligently copied the Bible. Sometimes they copied an entire book in beautiful scrolls, and sometimes they copied a verse or two on little scraps of parchment. But they copied it so often that today we have tens of thousands of source documents that enable us to reasonably reconstruct the original. We have such confidence in the Bible exactly because it spread so far so fast. And the gospel functions much the same. We guard the gospel by spreading it, by proclaiming it to everyone we encounter. The farther it spreads, the more difficult it is to twist it or lose it. So spread that gospel to everyone you encounter — your family first, your friends, your neighbors, your coworkers, and even outright strangers.

MISSIONS

Before he ascended to heaven, Jesus commissioned his disciples to take the gospel to the ends of the earth (Matthew 28:18–20; Acts 1:8). God uses such work for the purpose of displaying his glory for the joy of every tribe, tongue, people group, and nation (Psalm 67:1–7; Revelation 5:9–10). Therefore, Christians are to share the good news of Jesus nearby to their neighbors and beyond to the nations (Matthew 22:39; 24:14). In this way, the glad-hearted knowledge of God will spread throughout the world, overcoming every resistance (Habakkuk 2:14; Matthew 16:18).

For further study, see:
Operation World: The Definitive Prayer Guide to Every Nation by Jason Mandryk

God means to glorify himself by and through the gospel. We are God's plan for accomplishing that. He has no backup. He means for the good and pure gospel to spread from one person to another until it has spread over the entire earth. Christian, this is God's charge to you. He has given you his gospel and called you to steward it. Will you?

CONCLUSION

Our God is good and gracious, and he has given us an immeasurable number of gifts. He has put us in this world to use them and to enjoy them to his glory. We enjoy them best and honor him most when we faithfully steward each one of them, using them in the ways God intends and in ways that bring glory to his name.

NOTES

1. Greg Oden uses a similar outline in his book *Discipleship Essentials: A Guide to Building Your Life in Christ*, rev. ed. (Downers Grove, IL: InterVarsity, 2007).
2. Alberto Cairo, *The Functional Art* (Berkeley, CA: New Riders, 2013), 9 – 10.
3. Dane Ortlund, "What's All This 'Gospel-Centered' Talk About?" *Boundless.org*, July 14, 2014, www.boundless.org/faith/2014/whats-all-this-gospel-centered-talk-about (accessed July 31, 2015).
4. C. J. Mahaney, *Living the Cross-Centered Life* (Colorado Springs: Multnomah, 2006), 132.
5. Wayne Grudem, *Systematic Theology: An Introduction to Biblical Doctrine* (Grand Rapids: Zondervan, 1994), 954.
6. Ibid., 996.
7. See ibid., 842.
8. It may be helpful to read Tim Challies, *The Next Story: Faith, Friends, Family and the Digital World*, rev. ed. (Grand Rapids: Zondervan, 2015).
9. As I wrote this section, I was inspired by Gavin Ortlund's reflections on the Bible ("What Kind of a Thing Is the Bible? 6 Theses," December 26, 2014, http://gavinortlund.com/2014/12/26/what-kind-of-a-thing-is-the-bible-6-theses/ [accessed August 3, 2015]).
10. Ortlund, "What Kind of a Thing Is the Bible?"
11. See Bryan Chapell, *Christ-Centered Preaching: Redeeming the Expository Sermon* (Grand Rapids: Baker, 2005), 282.
12. I am no master of alliteration, so I can't help but wonder if I inadvertently absorbed this from another source. But all of my searches have come up empty.
13. Tim Keller, *Prayer: Experiencing Awe and Intimacy with God* (New York: Dutton, 2014), 55.
14. The term "peaceful adoration" comes from Keller, *Prayer*, 3.
15. Keller, *Prayer*, 43.
16. The term "assertive supplication" comes from Keller, *Prayer*, 3.
17. Michael Horton, *The Christian Faith: A Systematic Theology for Pilgrims on the Way* (Grand Rapids: Zondervan, 2011), 19.
18. Thomas Watson, *A Body of Divinity: Contained in Sermons upon the Westminster Assembly's Catechism* (1692; repr., Edinburgh: Banner of Truth, 2012), 4.
19. C. S. Lewis, *God in the Dock* (1970; repr., Grand Rapids: Eerdmans, 2014), 223.
20. *Westminster Shorter Catechism*, Q&A 14, www.shortercatechism.com/resources/wsc/wsc_014.html (accessed August 6, 2015).
21. John Owen, *Overcoming Sin and Temptation*, ed. Kelly M. Kapic and Justin Taylor, rev. ed. (Wheaton, IL: Crossway, 2015).
22. Heath Lambert, *Finally Free: Fighting for Purity with the Power of Grace* (Grand Rapids: Zondervan, 2013), 35.
23. Ibid., 27.
24. Thomas Brooks, *Precious Remedies Against Satan's Devices* (Philadelphia: Jonathan Pounder, 1810), 33.

25. R. C. Sproul, *The Holiness of God*, rev. ed. (Wheaton, IL: Tyndale, 1998), 33.
26. Gene Edward Veith, "Our Calling and God's Glory," *Modern Reformation* 16, no. 6 (November/December 2007), www.modernreformation.org/default.php?page= articledisplay&var2=881 (accessed August 6, 2015).
27. Ibid.
28. Ibid.
29. Gene Edward Veith, "The Doctrine of Vocation: How God Hides Himself in Human Work," *Modern Reformation* 8, no. 3 (May/June 1999), www.modernreformation.org/default.php?page=articledisplay&var2=541%20%20God%20Hides%E2%80%A6 (accessed August 6, 2015).
30. Ibid.
31. Randy Alcorn, *The Treasure Principle: Unlocking the Secret of Joyful Giving* (Colorado Springs: Multnomah, 2001), 18.
32. Noël Piper, *Faithful Women and their Extraordinary God* (Wheaton, IL: Crossway, 2005), 166.
33. Francis A. Schaeffer and Udo Middlemann, *Pollution and the Death of Man* (1970; repr., Wheaton, IL: Crossway, 2011), 71.